ALEISTER CROWLEY'S TREASURE HOUSE OF IMAGES

By Aleister Crowley and J. F. C. Fuller

**With contributions by David Cheribum,
Lon Milo DuQuette and Nancy Wasserman**

OCCULT CLASSICS

Some Other Titles From New Falcon Publications

Aha! The Sevenfold Mystery of the Ineffable Love **By Aleister Crowley**
Bio-Etheric Healing **By Trudy Lanitis**
Undoing Yourself With Energized Meditation and Other Devices
Secrets of Western Tantra: The Sexuality of the Middle Path
Dogma Daze **By Christopher S. Hyatt, Ph.D.**
Rebels & Devils; The Psychology of Liberation **Edited by Christopher S. Hyatt, Ph.D.**
Aleister Crowley's Illustrated Goetia
Taboo: Sex, Religion & Magick
Sex Magic, Tantra & Tarot: The Way of the Secret Lover
By Christopher S. Hyatt, Ph.D., and Lon Milo DuQuette
Pacts With The Devil
Urban Voodoo: A Beginner's Guide to Afro-Caribbean Magic
By Jason Black and Christopher S. Hyatt, Ph.D.
The Psychopath's Bible **By Christopher S. Hyatt, Ph.D., and Jack Willis**
Ask Baba Lon **By Lon Milo DuQuette**
Aleister Crowley and the Treasure House of Images **By J.F.C. Fuller, Aleister Crowley, Lon Milo DuQuette and Nancy Wasserman**
Enochian World of Aleister Crowley **By Lon Milo DuQuette and Aleister Crowley**

Info-Psychology   Neuropolitique   The Game of Life
What Does WoMan Want? **By Timothy Leary, Ph.D.**

Be Yourself - A Guide to Relaxation and Health
Dr. Israel Regardie's Definitive Work on Aleister Crowley, The Eye In The Triangle
Healing Energy, Prayer and Relaxation
My Rosicrucian Adventure
Teachers of Fulfillment
The Complete Golden Dawn System of Magic
The Eye in the Triangle: An Interpretation of Aleister Crowley
The Golden Dawn Audio CDs
The Legend of Aleister Crowley
The Portable Complete Golden Dawn System of Magic
The Tree of Life
What You Should Know About the Golden Dawn **By Dr. Israel Regardie**

Roll Away The Stone/The Herb Dangerous **By Israel Regardie and Aleister Crowley**

Rebellion, Revolution and Religiousness **By Osho**
Reichian Therapy: A PracticalGuide for Home Use **By Dr. Jack Willis**
Woman's Orgasm: A Guide to Sexual Satisfaction **By Benjamin Graber, M.D., and Georgia Kline-Graber, R.N.**
Shaping Formless Fire   Seizing Power   Taking Power **By Stephen Mace**
The Illuminati Conspiracy: The Sapiens System **By Donald Holmes, M.D.**
The Secret Inner Order Rituals of the Golden Dawn **By Pat Zalewski**

MANY OF OUR TITLES AVAILABLE ON KINDLE!
Please visit our website at http://www.newfalcon.com

ALEISTER CROWLEY'S TREASURE HOUSE OF IMAGES

By Aleister Crowley and J. F. C. Fuller

With contributions by David Cheribum, Lon Milo DuQuette and Nancy Wasserman

OCCULT CLASSICS

NEW FALCON PUBLICATIONS
Los Angeles, California

Copyright ©1994, 2010 and 2020 New Falcon Publications

All rights reserved. No part of this book,
in part or in whole, may be reproduced, transmitted,
or utilized, in any form or by any means, electronic or mechanical,
including photocopying, recording, or by any information storage
and retrieval system, without permission in writing
from the publisher, except for brief quotations
in critical articles, books and reviews.

ISBN 13: 978-1-56184-569-9
ISBN 10: 1-56184-569-8

First published in 1994 as
The Pathworkings of Aleister Crowley

New Falcon Publications Occult Classics First Edition 2020

The paper used in this publication meets the minimum requirements
of the American National Standard for Permanence of
Paper for Printed Library Materials Z39.48-1984

Printed in USA

NEW FALCON PUBLICATIONS
2046 HILLHURST AVE., ROOM 23
LOS ANGELES, CA 90027
www.newfalcon.com
email: info@newfalcon.com

J. F. C. Fuller *circa* 1919

Table of Contents

Foreword to the New Edition Lon Milo DuQuette		1
Introduction David Cherubim		9
Liber DCCCCLXIII J. F. C. Fuller and Aleister Crowley		23
Chapter 1	The Perception of God	31
Chapter 2	The Twelvefold Affirmation of God	33
Chapter 3	The Twelvefold Renunciation of God	35
Chapter 4	The Twelvefold Conjuration of God	39
Chapter 5	The Twelvefold Certitude of God	41
Chapter 6	The Twelvefold Glorification of God	45
Chapter 7	The Twelvefold Beseechment of God	47
Chapter 8	The Twelvefold Gratification of God	49
Chapter 9	The Twelvefold Denial of God	51
Chapter 10	The Twelvefold Rejoicing of God	57
Chapter 11	The Twelvefold Humiliation of God	63

Table of Contents continued

Chapter 12	The Twelvefold Lamentation of God	65
Chapter 13	The Twelvefold Bewilderment of God	69
Chapter 14	The Twelvefold Unification of God	73
Chapter 15	The Hundred and Sixty-Nine Cries of Adoration of God	77
Chapter 16	The Unconscious of God	93

Afterword: Pathworking Practice — 101
Nancy Wasserman

Liber O vel Manus et Sagittae — 113
Alesiter Crowley

Illustrations

Major-General J. F. C. Fuller	*Frontispiece*
Magical Square	24
The Triangle of the Universe	25
The Greek Cross of the Zodiac	97
Tree of Life	99
The Sign of the Enterer (Blind Force)	113
The Signs of the Grades	121-123
The Sign of Silence (Silent Watcher)	133

Foreword to the New Edition
Lon Milo DuQuette

"It has taken 100,000 years to produce Aleister Crowley. The world has indeed laboured, and has at last brought forth a man."
—*Capt. J. F. C. Fuller*[1]

The Convert
(A Hundred Years Hence)

There met one eve in a sylvan glade
A horrible Man and a beautiful maid.
"Where are you going, so meek and holy?"
"I'm going to temple to worship Crowley."
"Crowley is God, then? How did you know?"
"Why, it Captain Fuller that told us so."
"And how do you know that Fuller was right?"
"I'm afraid you're a wicked man; Good-night."

While this sort of thing is styled success
I shall not count failure bitterness.
                    —*Aleister Crowley*[2]

Do what thou wilt shall be the whole of the Law.

Aleister Crowley's Treasure House of Images is the title of this little book, but a quick glance at its contents might cause the reader to prematurely conclude there is precious little Aleister Crowley in it. Indeed,

---

[1] Capt. J. F. C. Fuller. *The Star in the West–A Critical Essay on the Works of Aleister Crowley*. Originally published in 1907 by The Walter Scott Company, New York and numerous subsequent editions, p. 211.

[2] Originally published in *The Winged Beetle*. (London: Elkin Mathews, 1910). Published most recently with introduction by Martin P Starr (Chicago: The Teitan Press, Inc., 1992). p. 102.

where the actual text of the *Treasure House of Images* itself is concerned only the "*Note Upon Liber DCCCCLXIII*" that immediately follows the title page can be rightly attributed to Crowley's pen.

I grant you, it's an important note–so important, in fact, that he classified it an "A∴A∴ Publication in Class A," and pronounced it among the works "…which may be changed not so much as the style of a letter; that is, they represent the utterance of an Adept entirely beyond the criticism of even the Visible Head of the Organization." The fact remains, however, *Aleister Crowley's Treasure House of Images* itself is the utterance not of the prophet but of the prophet's herald–the first disciple to formally subscribe to Crowley's program of Scientific Illuminism, and arguably for a number of years his most enthusiastic supporter.

John Frederick Charles Fuller (1878-1966) was an infantry officer of the Indian Army, later to become Major-General Fuller, C.B. C.B.E., D.S.O. An expert on tank warfare, Fuller's military writings would, in his long and distinguished career, earn him the respect of friends and enemies alike. In 1939 Fuller received the awkward distinction of being one of only two Englishmen invited by Adolph Hitler to the celebration of the German dictator's 50th birthday.

Crowley and Fuller came together in the most spectacular fashion. In 1907 when the third and final volume of *The Collected Works of Aleister Crowley* appeared, Crowley advertised a promotional competition: "The Chance of the Year! The Chance of the Century! The Chance of the Geologic Period!" He offered a prize of £100 for the best critical essay on his writings. Fuller entered the contest and was the prize-winner with his 327 page essay, *The Star in the West*. It is unclear whether Fuller ever actually received the £100, but it was the beginning of what would become for a few golden years a beautiful friendship.

Not everyone agrees that Aleister Crowley was a holy prophet or the Logos of the New Aeon. However, few knowledgeable critics would deny that he possessed sufficient second-sight to foretell the specter of future cults of personality that would inevitably form around his name, his work, and (most ironically) his character. Not that he was particularly opposed to the idea of a little guru-worship during his lifetime, but only in the context of the disciplinary relationship necessary for those who voluntarily enlisted in any program of personally supervised spiritual development. For his personal students there was indeed a heavy element of 'Obey me!' in the Great Beast's program. However, in matters concerning his doctrines, his philosophy, his magick, and his (if we dare use the word) religion, his uncompromising admonition was a firmly consistent and unambiguous "Don't believe me!"

Crowley hated the idea of 'true believers' yet at the same time was utterly flabbergasted that any moderately intelligent person would not immediately see the brilliance of his message. Sadly, there would be few in his lifetime that would be able to see beyond the blinding glare of certain colorful aspects of the messenger's outrageous character. This fact, more than any other, is perhaps the most tragic aspect of the life of this remarkable man.

Fuller, on the other hand, was anything but outrageous, but for a time he was that rarest combination of true believer and independent thinker. His admiration for Crowley's poetry, magick, philosophy, and personality transcended that of the fanatic or hero worshiper–precisely the kind of reaction Crowley naively expected from everyone who came in contact with his work. Indeed, it is clear to me that even before their relationship began Fuller was already a fuel-packed tinderbox of creativity just waiting for a catalyst–an ignition spark of sufficient heat to detonate his soul into a raging Sun. Aleister Crowley would be that spark.

The mystic can argue (if mystics actually spend their time arguing) that Fuller's dharma was such that any number of catalytic events could have served to light the fuse to the young captain's Roman candle. Perhaps this is so. But there is an additional factor in this equation that renders must that argument–an intangible yet vital manifestation of divine spirit that cannot be comprehended by the machinery of our meat brains or adequately discussed with our words and images; a Goddess whose presence or absence spells life or death to the artist. I am, of course, speaking about that most personal and elusive of deities known by Her most generic title "Muse." For a sacred season these two remarkable men simultaneously functioned as each other's Muse.

Such events are not without precedence in mythological tradition. After all, John the Baptist said of Jesus, "Behold the lamb of God!" and Jesus repaid the compliment by telling the world, "Verily I say unto you, Among them that are born of women there hath not risen a greater than John the Baptist." As a live microphone placed too near a live amplifier will feed back a loop ever-increasing sound volume, so too the Muse of Crowley fed and amplified the genius of Fuller and the Muse of Crowley fed and amplified the genius of Crowley. The 'feed-back' that was created resulted in one of the most spiritually productive periods in each man's life, and a body of work of unparalleled beauty and profundity.

Fuller's study of Crowley (in which he boldly coined the term "Crowleyanity") was an unabashed and undiluted love song to things Crowley. In the years to follow Fuller would continue to reward his idol with literary labors that filled the pages of Crowley's periodical, *The Equinox*. Foremost among these efforts was *Aleister Crowley's Treasure House of Images*.

Crowley in turn rewarded Fuller by dedicating in gushing verse an entire collection of poems, *The Winged Beetle*, to the young captain.

> I DEDICATE THIS COLLECTION OF POEMS TO
> JOHN FREDERICK CHARLES FULLER
> DEDICATION

> Out of the East, out of the East,
>   Didst thou flame forth, O Son of Man,
> The chainless champion of the Beast!
>   A warrior comet, thy plumes fan
> The shuddering air's black wildernesses
> To fiend's insatiate caresses.

Thou camest crowned and helmed and armed,
  Sworded, a mighty man of war:
Swayed all the stars, aghast, alarmed
  As at the Thunderbolt of Thor!
The very Aethyr rocked and shook
At thine indomitable look!

[Here must we utterly restrict
  Our theological remarks,
One whom not Heaven could contradict
  Says: Now, Sir, if you please, no larks!
Hence for third stanza (with a curse)
I write instead this sorry verse.]

Yea, with one song of starry flame
  In brilliance of immortal youth
Didst thou stand steadfast and proclaim
  Freedom and Ecstasy and Truth,
Erect amid the wreck of Things
Poised on inexorable wings!

So much the universe may see
  When its bat's-eyes may endure the sun:
This secret rests my prize to me,
  That I knew thee, surpassed of none,
Fighting and faithful to the end,
A perfect knight, a perfect friend.

Like he did to nearly everyone who loved and respected him, Crowley eventually drove Fuller away. But for a few remarkable years Fuller was indeed for Crowley *a perfect knight, a perfect friend*.

Aleister Crowley's Treasure House of Images was Fuller's inspired creation, but it will also forever be part of Crowley's legacy. Today, all over the world, O.T.O.[3] bodies mount public productions of Crowley's seven Rites of Eleusis and throughout the series audiences are treated to eight full zodiacal chapters by Fuller in *Aleister Crowley's Treasure House of Images*, recited, chanted, and sung and arranged for orchestra.

Even though these Rites of Eleusis have no historic or orthodox connection to the ancient Greek mystery school, they nonetheless were fashioned to evoke the same response in the minds, hearts and souls of the participants–the willed elevation of consciousness. Ask anyone who has been fortunate enough to be a part of one or more of these irrationally beautiful ritual plays and you are likely to hear that the experience does just that.

It is my sincere wish that you also will choose to experience a willed elevation of consciousness and heed the instructions outlined in Crowley's Class A document, *A Note Upon Liber DCCCCLXIII*, and use the magick incantations of the *Treasure House of Images* to enflame yourself in the adoration of your star.

I can think of no better way to close this brief Foreword than by letting both men speak of themselves. On the next two pages, I hereby append the closing words from Fuller's *The Star in the West*. Crowley's quote is in italics.

Love, is the law, love under will.

From *The Star in the West*

At last we have arrived at the close of a difficult yet intensely interesting journey. Crowleyanity has led us through more marvels than Dante ever bore witness to in the "Paradiso" and the "Inferno." His may have

---

[3] *Ordo Templi Orientis* (Order of the Temple of the East, or the Order of Oriental Templars) is an international fraternal and religious organization founded at the beginning of the 20th century. Originally it was intended to be modeled after and association with Freemasonry, but under the leadership of Aleister Crowley was a reorganized as a non Masonic organization based on the Law of Thelema as its central religious principle. This Law–expressed as "Do what thou wilt shall be the whole of the Law" and "Love is the law, love under will"–was established in 1904 with the dictation of *The Book of Law*.

been a Divine Comedy, but here before us has been unrolled the vast drama of a Sublime Tragedy: "All arguments are arguments in a circle," and there is a home to which we all one day shall have to return, to the celestial home of crowning glory. Some spur and spare not, others linger, and others dawdle in the by-ways and lanes of existence, yet the most tardy will one day catch up with the fastest and a time will come when the tortoise will be one with the hare. All is one, either a mass of impressions (Locke, Hume), or a mass of consciousness (Berkeley and Fichte), all is unity, controversy is verbal, dispute the more beating of the winds with a tattered fan. Religion is bankrupt, philosophy is bankrupt, science is bankrupt, none will be discharged, we must fend for ourselves…Hark!

We are the poets! We are the children of wood and stream, of mist and mountains, of sun and wind! We adore the moon and the stars, and go into the London streets at midnight seeking Their kisses as our birthright. We are the Greeks–and God grant ye all, my brothers, to be as happy in your loves! and to us the rites of Eleusis should open the door of Heaven, and we shall enter and see God face to face.

…

Under the stars I go forth, my brothers, and drink of that lustral dew: I will return, my brothers, when I have seen God face to face, and read within those eternal eyes the secret that shall make you free.

Then will I choose you and test you and instruct you in the Mysteries of Eleusis, oh ye brave hearts, and cool eyes, and trembling lips! I will put a live coal upon your lips, and flowers upon your eyes, and a sword in your hearts, and ye also shall see God face to face.

Thus shall we give back its youth to the world, for like tongues of triple flames we shall brood upon the Great Deep–Hail unto the Lords of the Groves of Eleusis![4]

That which was to be said hereon is spoken. Amen without lie, Amen and Amen of Amen.[5]

---

[4] *Eleusis*. From The Collected Works of Aleister Crowley, vol. iii, pp. 229, 230.
[5] Op. cit. pp. 326, 327.

INTRODUCTION
DAVID CHERUBIM

> "O Thou Unity of all things: as the Sun
> that rolleth through the twelve mansions
> of the skies, so art Thou, O God my God.
> I cannot slay Thee, for Thou art everywhere;
> lo! though I lick up the Boundless Light,
> the Boundless, and the Not, there shall I
> find Thee, Thou Unity of Unities, Thou
> Oneness, O Thou perfect Nothingness of Bliss!"
> –*Capt. J. F. C. Fuller*

Do what thou wilt shall be the whole of the Law.

Aleister Crowley's Treasure House of Images is a priceless work of precious prose. It contains thirteen chapters of exquisite hymns to the twelve signs of the Zodiac and the Sun. Each chapter of hymns contains thirteen sections. Each of these thirteen sections has the same number of syllables. Moreover, in each section one zodiacal sign is modified by another sign. There is also a chapter containing one hundred and sixty-nine cries of adoration. This chapter, called "The Hundred and Sixty-nine Cries of Adoration of God and the Unity thereof" is a multiplication and quintessentialization of the previous chapters. In his Autohagiography (*The Confessions of Aleister Crowley*), the magician Aleister Crowley said that *The Treasure House of Images* is, formally, the most remarkable prose that has ever been written. He also stated that it is the most astonishing achievement in symbolism.

The Treasure House of Images was composed by one of Aleister Crowley's most important disciples, a man named Captain, later Major-General, J. F. C. Fuller (John Frederick Charles Fuller) of the Oxfordshire Light Infantry. He was the first person to join and pledge himself a student of A∴A∴, the Magical Order announced in 1907 E.V. by Crowley and George Cecil Jones. It was Fuller who, in 1909 E.V., suggested to Crowley that he meet with an associate of his named Victor Neuburg, who was to become one of Crowley's most devoted disciples and his partner in several critically important magical workings.

Aleister Crowley's Treasure House of Images was originally published as a special supplement to *The Equinox*, Vol. I, No. III (March 1910 E.V.). *The Equinox* is the Official Organ of the A∴A∴, known as the Review of Scientific Illuminism. Later, in his Autohagiography, Crowley made the remark that Fuller reached his high-water mark with *The Treasure House of Images*.

Some of the chapters of hymns in *Aleister Crowley's Treasure House of Images* were incorporated by Crowley in his planetary *Rites of Eleusis* performed for the public in 1910 E.V. at Caxton Hall, Westminster. (See *Equinox* Vol. I, No. VI.) For example, the chapter called "The Twelvefold Glorification of God and the Unity thereof," which pertains to the sign of Leo, was recited in the Rite of Sol, since Leo is ruled by the Sun; "The Twelvefold Certitude of God and the Unity thereof," which pertains to the sign of Cancer, was recited in the Rite of Luna since Cancer is ruled by the Moon.

In "A Syllabus of the Official Instructions of (See *Equinox*, Vol. I, No. X, or *Gems from the Equinox* (Weiser), Crowley listed *The Treasure House of Images* (*Liber* 963) as Class A and B in the classification system of the A∴A∴. This book contains a short prefatory note which his in Class A, whereas the book itself is in Class B.

The following is Crowley's description of the classification system of the A∴A∴:

"The publications of the A∴A∴ divide themselves into four classes.

"Class A consists of books of which may be changed not so much as the style of a letter; that is, they represent the utterance of an Adept entirely beyond the criticism of even the Visible Head of the Organization.

"Class B consists of books or essays which are the result of ordinary scholarship, enlightened and earnest.

"Class C consists of matter which is to be regarded rather as suggestive than anything else.

"Class D consists of the Official Rituals and Instructions.

"Some publications are composite, and pertain to more than one class."

It should be noted that a fifth class (Class E) came into use in 1919 E.V. Crowley classified under Class E manifestos, broadsides, epistles and other public statements.

The Treasure House of Images was issued in *The Equinox* under the numerical figure of DCCCCLXIII or CMLXIII (963). 963 is the numerical value of the Hebrew "OTRTh OTRH" (עטרת עטרה) which means "A Garland, Crown; a little wreath." 963 is also the numerical value of the Hebrew "AChAD" (אחד) spelt in full (אלף חיתדלת). Achad is a Hebrew word meaning "Unity." *The Treasure House of Images* is otherwise called *The Book of the Meditations on the Twelvefold Adoration, and the Unity of God*. The whole gist of this book of hymns is Unity.

Now consider the following information, which, if properly interpreted, should open for you new portals to the Palace of Wisdom, enlightening your understanding and perfecting your knowledge of Self whose very nature is Unity.

On the Qabalistic Tree of Life, Unity is symbolized by the first Sephira called Kether. (See the illustration of the Tree of Life on page 99.) Kether is a Hebrew word which means "the Crown." Kether represents the True Self, the Yechidah of Qabalistic Philosophy.

Tiphareth, the sixth Sephira on the Tree of Life, is the reflection of Kether or the True Self in the mind of man. Tiphareth is the Sphere of the Sun, and the Sun is a visible sign of an invisible Grace. In other words, it is an outward sign of the nature of Kether, the Qabalistic symbol of the True Self. The Sun is also the Lord of the Solar System, and of the twelve signs of the Zodiac. As mentioned earlier, *Liber 963* contains hymns to the Sun and the twelve signs of the Zodiac.

These twelve zodiacal signs are the archetypal images of our own celestial natures; they represent our own Universal Identities, our archetypal centers of expression for the current of the Universal Will. They are the various aspects of our Universal Self (Yechidah), and they comprise the unity of our being. They are the twelve cosmic modes of solar expression, being the twelve rays of the Sun of Kether.

Through these twelve rays the Sun expresses and experiences itself as a Unity. These twelve zodiacal rays are what constitute the unity of our True Self represented by the Sun. To understand this Self aright, we should not think of it in an Aristotelian or Hindu static sense, in the form of an essence which never changes and is eternally one. We must rather conceive of it as a dynamic multidimensional Self which is really not a self at all. We have a variety of different potential selves rather than one unchanging Self; and we are only one in essence when we are expressing all of our potential selves. These potential selves are represented in Astrology by the twelve signs of the Zodiac. These signs comprise what we may rightfully term the Astrological Self, which is simply another name for our Universal or Multidimensional Self.

That which we so commonly call our True Self in the philosophy of Magick is not in "essence" a single self. Rather is it a multiple unit. It is only One insofar that it is Many. It is not a monistic or monotheistic reality of any commonly accepted sort; it is rather a polytheistic or multiple reality. We cannot assume any existential meaning when we analyze ourselves part by part. In the final analysis we can only conclude that we are a Unit of the various parts which constitute our manifold existence; and that our true individuality or Unity arises by expressing our Multidimensional or Astrological Self, fulfilling all of our possibilities.

From a Thelemic point of view, let us consider that Hadit, the central core of our being, is not a static principle; He is rather in constant motion, fulfilling all of His possibilities in Nuit. Without Nuit, Hadit is a meaningless principle. Now Hadit is the Sun, a unit of the Macrocosm or a single point concentrating Space, and Nuit is identifiable with the twelve signs of the Zodiac which represent in Astrology the Macrocosm or Universe. The Sun expresses and experiences itself as a unity through the twelve signs; or, in other terms, Hadit fulfills himself by combining with Nuit for the birth of Ra-Hoor-Khuit who represents, in Thelemic Qabalah, a unity which includes and heads all things, or a "Unity of Unities."

The Sun of Unity is only such by way of his being the Many. One in itself means nothing. Life demands multiplicity of expression. Only thus can true integration be achieved. Unity or oneness is a meaningless reality without multiplicity. It has been said that "All is a mask of the One." It is more appropriate in this place to say that THE ONE IS A MASK OF THE ALL.

If we are to truly understand and experience the unity of the Sun of Kether, we need to banish that old demon of monistic thinking and stop interpreting god, self or reality as one, replacing this ancient linear and self-centered belief with a new vision of seeing things in a multidimensional manner. This we must do if we are to genuinely realize the One in the midst of the All, to attain the sublime starry consciousness of Kether, and to truly live in the joy and rapture of Unity, or to become an integrated individual or, more accurately yet more paradoxically, a multiple unit or multidimensional monad. This multiple unit is symbolized by the Sun, the visible sign of Kether (Unity).

Now the hymns of *Liber 963* can be used as a method to adore the various parts or facets which constitute our starry unit of Space and to adore the Sun, the visible symbol of Kether, the Crown. To adore is to unite, to integrate with a particular deity, principle or force of Nature. The hymns in Liber 963 can be used to adore the various facets of our starry unit, those parts of our Self which constitute our Oneness and which are symbolized by the twelve signs of the Zodiac. But we are in fact a synthesis or Unity of all twelve signs; and to focus upon one to the exclusion of the others, as is most often the case, is to live in the deadly delusion that you are One without the necessary experiential understanding of the many factors which constitute your Oneness.

It is written that the Probationer of the A∴A∴ should learn by heart the chapter in Liber 963 that corresponds to the zodiacal sign that was rising at his birth; or, if this be unknown, the chapter called "The Twelve-fold Unification of God and the Unity thereof" which pertains to the Sun. The Probationer (Grade $0° = 0°$) is not yet an initiated member of the A∴A∴, but seeks to become such after a necessary probationary period of at least one year. He is bound by Oath to prosecute the Great Work which is, in his particular case, the task of obtaining a scientific knowledge of the nature and powers of his own being.

The zodiacal sign that was rising at his birth is the sign of the Ascendant in his astrological horoscope. The Ascendant is the place on the horoscope where the Sun is located at sunrise, and it is the point of individual self-hood and self-awareness; it indicates by its sign and degree the Probationer as a self-conscious entity; it is the most personal factor in his horoscope. The sign of the Ascendent, or the sign rising over the eastern horizon at the time of his birth, is significant of the nature and powers of his own being. Thus to memorize and apply the chapter that corresponds to his Rising Sign serves to contribute to the fulfillment of his Oath, preparing him for initiation in the A∴A∴, to become a Neophyte and commence the process of ascending the Tree of Initiation.

In "*A Note upon Liber DCCCCLXIII*" we read the following:

1. Let the student recite this book, particularly the 169 Adorations, unto his Star as it ariseth.

2. Let him seek out diligently in the sky his Star; let him travel thereunto in his Shell; let him adore it unceasingly from its rising even unto its setting by the right adorations, with chants that shall be harmonious therewith.

3. Let him rock himself to and fro in adoration; let him spin around his own axis in adoration; let him leap up and down in adoration.

4. Let him inflame himself in the adoration, speeding from slow to fast, until he can no more.

5. This also shall be sung in open places, as heaths, mountains, woods, and by streams and upon islands.

6. Moreover, ye shall build you fortified places in great cities, caverns and tombs shall be made glad with your praise.

7. Amen.

We are, of course, free to interpret as we will the Star referred to in "*A Note upon Liber DCCCCLXIII*." First we shall freely interpret it as the star of our horoscope, that is, the celestial body or planet that rules our Rising Sign. The planets, particularly among the ancient astrologers, were often called stars. The planet which rules the sign of the Ascendent is the star of an individual's life and it exerts the greatest influence upon him. Thus it is called in astrology the Lord of the Horoscope.

Now if, for instance, your Rising Sign were Leo, the Sun would be your star to which you are to travel in your Shell (Astral Body) and adore with the 169 Adorations and other appropriate litanies which, in this case, would be found in "The Chapter known as the Twelvefold Unification of God and the Unity thereof" since this chapter pertains to the Sun. Or you may recite "The Chapter known as The Twelvefold Glorification of God and the Unity thereof" since this chapter pertains to the sign of Leo which is ruled by the Sun.

Or if, for instance, your Rising Sign were Aquarius, Saturn would be your star and the appropriate litanies would be found in "The Chapter known as The Twelvefold Lamentation of God and the Unity thereof" since this chapter pertains to the sign of Aquarius and to Saturn, which traditionally rules the sign of Aquarius.

We are also free to interpret this star in a more esoteric sense, referring it to our own personal star (or Unit of Space) in one of the constellations of a zodiacal sign. In *The Book of Law*, Chapter 1, Verse 3, Nuit, Our Lady of the Stars, indeed proclaims "Every man and every woman is a star." *In The Law is for All* (Thelema Media), Crowley stated that there may be some real connection between a given person and a given star. In certain forms of both ancient and modern mythology, the stars are linked with Angelic beings. This is a very curious connection in respect of the fact that in the philosophy of Thelema we view our star as our Holy Guardian Angel. This Angel, or Start, is our own Inmost Self. It is who we are in truth, a Sun or single concentration of Nuit, a celestial unit of Infinite Space. To seek out and travel to this Star in your Shell is to discover its appropriate location in the Heavens, that is, in the appropriate constellation of stars, and to travel thereunto in your Astral Body of Light.

It should be noted that in Astrology the stars are often called "fixed," referring to the fact that they do not traverse the signs of the Zodiac as do the planets. There are no actual stars located in the Zodiac. The stars are a part of the constellations beyond the Zodiac. The constellations and the signs have the same names, but they are not the same thing. The Zodiac of constellations is a group of fixed stars and is called the "Sidereal Zodiac," whereas the Zodiac of signs is called the "Tropical Zodiac." The Tropical Zodiac and the Sidereal Zodiac were, at one time, the same; but at the present time it is estimated that they are approximately 24 degrees apart.

Pathworking is a method of rising in your Body of Light to a chosen place or Path in the Astral Plane. The Astral Plane is called the World of Yetzirah in Qabalistic Philosophy. The Treasure House of Images is another name for the Astral World in which is contained the Yetziratic

Tree of Life. A Pathworking is generally done by ascending the Yetziratic Tree of Life in your Astral Body to a particular Path on the Tree. The twelve signs of the Zodiac pertain to twelve of the Paths on the Tree of Life. The planets which rule these signs also pertain to certain Paths on the Tree. (See illustration of the Tree of Life on page 99.) The Paths are the twenty-two connecting links between the ten Sephiroth or circular spheres. These twenty-two Paths correspond with the twenty-two Hebrew letters and the twenty-two Major Arcana of Tarot or Atu of Thoth.

Now if, for instance, you wanted to perform a Pathworking for the sign of Leo, you would travel to the Path of Teth (Path 19) on the Yetziratic Tree of Life, which connects the two Sephiroth called Chesed (4) and Geburah (5), and which pertains to the Sign of Leo and the Atu of Thoth called "Lust" (Atu XI). Or if, for instance, you wanted to travel to the Path of the Sun, you would perform a working for the Path of Resh (Path 30), which connects the two Sephiroth called Hod (8) and Yesod (9), and which pertains to the Sun and to the Atu of Thoth called "The Sun" (Atu XIX).

To correctly perform a Pathworking it is necessary to know the symbols and meanings of not only the Path and the Sephiroth of the Tree of Life, but also the Tarot Atu of Thoth. These Atu are the Major Arcana (Major Secrets) of Tarot, numbered 0-XXI, commencing with the Atu called "The Fool" and ending with the Atu called "The Universe."

For operational Pathworking, the Atu of Thoth are used as Keys, metaphorically speaking, by which to enter a Path on the Yetziratic Tree of Life. The Atu of Thoth are linked subconsciously with the twelve Astrological signs, the Sun, Moon and the planets. The symbolism of the Atu can be used by the student as a direct means to attune his astral consciousness to the twelve zodiacal signs and their ruling planets, to obtain a vision of their nature, and to develop a greater understanding of their relationship to himself as a Unity thereof.

We shall now list the twelve signs of the Zodiac, their corresponding Tarot cards (Atu of Thoth), and their ruling planet(s). Note that the Sun and Moon are often termed planets, though technically the Sun is a star and the Moon is a satellite.

Sign	Tarot Atu	Ruling Planet
Aries	Atu IV (The Emperor)	Mars, Pluto
Taurus	Atu V (The Hierophant)	Venus
Gemini	Atu VI (The Lovers)	Mercury
Cancer	Atu VII (The Chariot)	Moon
Leo	Atu XI (Lust)	Sun
Virgo	Atu IX (The Hermit)	Mercury
Libra	Atu VIII (Adjustment)	Venus
Scorpio	Atu XIII (Death)	Pluto, Mars
Sagittarius	Atu XIV (Art)	Jupiter
Capricorn	Atu XV (The Devil)	Saturn
Aquarius	Atu XVII (The Star)	Uranus, Saturn
Pisces	Atu XVIII (The Moon)	Neptune, Jupiter

Where there are two planets listed above, it is due to the fact that Uranus, Neptune and Pluto were not recognized by the ancient astrologers and were not appointed by them as ruling planets of any of the twelve astrological signs. However, they are now appointed as such. Uranus was discovered in 1781 E.V., Neptune was discovered in 1846 E.V., and Pluto was discovered in 1930 E.V. Uranus is called the Higher Octave of Mercury; Neptune is called the Higher Octave of Venus; and Pluto is called the Higher Octave of Mars. When Uranus was discovered in 1781 by Sir William Herschel, it was predicted that two more planets would be discovered beyond Uranus and that they would be called Isis and Osiris are certainly appropriate names for these two mysterious planets, just as Horus, the Child of Isis and Osiris, is an appropriate name for the planet Uranus.

If it be your Will to perform a Pathworking to obtain a vision pertaining to a planet instead of an astrological sign, you would use one of the chapters of hymns in Liber 963 which pertains to a zodiacal sign ruled by the planet, and you would use the Atu of Thoth which corresponds with the planet. Thus, if it be your Will to adore Venus, you would use the hymns of either Taurus or Libra which are ruled by the planet Venus, and you would use the Atu of Thoth called "The Empress" which pertains to the planet Venus.

The planets have their own corresponding Atu of Thoth which can be used for operational Pathworkings. Such are the following:

Planet	**Tarot Atu**
Saturn	Atu XXI (The Universe)
Luna	Atu II (The Priestess)
Mercury	Atu I (The Magus)
Venus	Atu III (The Empress)
Sol	Atu XIX (The Sun)
Mars	Atu XVI (The Tower)
Jupiter	Atu X (Fortune)
Uranus	Atu 0 (The Fool)
Pluto	Atu XXI (The Aeon)
Neptune	Atu XII (The Hanged Man)

There are a number of magical techniques for operational Pathworkings, by which to travel to a chosen Path in the Astral World in your Shell or Body of Light. It will benefit the student to research these various techniques at length in such books that may be accessible to him. But we highly recommend you make a thorough study of Aleister Crowley's *Liber O vel Manus et Sagittae*, particularly section V. (*Liber O* is included at the end of the present volume.) The Afterword to this book by Nancy Wasserman provides a valuable guide to beginning your practice of Pathworking. We also suggest the student study the last two sections of Volume V of *The Complete Golden Dawn System of Magic*, by Israel Regardie (New Falcon Publications). Finally, see Chapter XVIII and

Appendix III of *Magick in Theory and Practice* by Aleister Crowley for information concerning the proper development of the Body of Light and the nature of the Astral Plane.

Here ends our introduction to *Aleister Crowley's Treasure House of Images*. May this book of precious hymns and adorations be unto you as a Sun of Light in your sublime quest for the attainment of True Unity, the Philosopher's Stone, the Summum Bonum, and Perfect Joy. *Sic sit vobis!*

Love is the law, love under will.

THE TREASURE HOUSE OF IMAGES

A∴A∴
Publication in Class B.
Issued by Order of
D.D.S. 7° = 4° Praemonstrator
O.S.V. 6° = 5° Imperator
N.F.S. 5° = 6° Cancellarius

LIBER
ΘΕΣΑΥΡΟΥ ἘΙΔΩΛΩΝ

SUB FIGURA
DCCCLXIII

צטרת צטרה

Corona, Corolla;
Sic vocatur Malchuth
quando ascendit usque
ad Kether

The Kabbala

(The Probationer should learn by heart the chapter corresponding to the Zodiacal Sign that was rising at his birth; or if this be unknown, the chapter "The Twelvefold Unification of God.")

93	108	123	138	153	168	1	16	31	46	61	76	91
107	122	137	152	167	13	15	30	45	60	75	90	92
121	136	151	166	12	14	29	44	59	74	89	104	106
135	150	165	11	26	28	43	58	73	88	103	105	120
149	164	10	25	27	42	57	72	87	102	117	119	134
163	9	24	39	41	56	71	86	101	116	118	133	148
8	23	38	40	55	70	85	100	115	130	132	147	162
22	37	52	54	69	84	99	114	129	131	146	161	7
36	51	53	68	83	98	113	128	143	145	160	6	21
50	65	67	82	97	112	127	142	144	159	5	20	35
64	66	81	96	111	126	141	156	158	4	19	34	49
78	80	95	110	125	140	155	157	3	18	33	48	63
79	94	109	124	139	154	169	2	17	32	47	62	77

The Magical Square

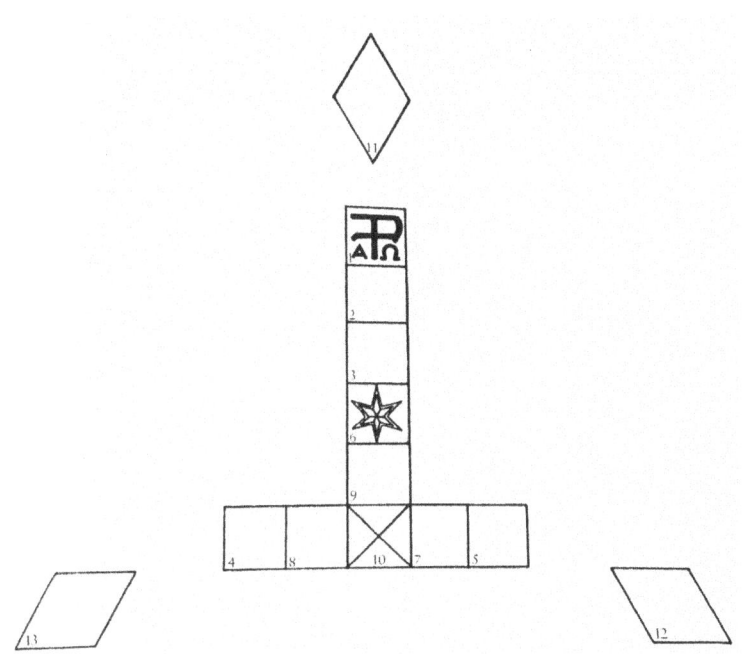

The Triangle of the Universe

Three veils of the Negative–not yellow; not red; not blue; but therefore symbolised by the "flashing" colours of these three; purple (11); emerald (12) and orange (13). Within their triangle of Yonis is the Lingam touching and filling it. Positive, as they are negative; in the Queen Scale of colour, as they are in the King Scale. Ten are the Emanations of Unity, the parts of that Lingam, in Kether, TARO= 78 = 6 x 13, the Influence of that Unity in the Macrocosm (Hexagram). The centre of the whole figure is Tiphereth, where is a golden Sun of six rays. Note the reflection of the Yonis to the triad about Malkuth. Also note that the triangle of Yonis is hidden, even as their links are secret. From Malkuth depends the Greek Cross of the Zodiac and their Spiritual Centre (See illustration on page 97). For Colour Scales see 777.

✺

A∴A∴
Publication in Class A.

A NOTE UPON LIBER DCCCCLXIII

1. Let the student recite this book, particularly the 169 Adorations, unto his Star as it ariseth.

2. Let him seek out diligently in the sky his Star; let him travel thereunto in his Shell; let him adore it unceasingly from its rising even unto its setting by the right adorations, with chants that shall be harmonious therewith.

3. Let him rock himself to and fro in adoration; let him spin around his own axis in adoration; let him leap up and down in adoration.

4. Let him inflame himself in the adoration, speeding from slow to fast, until he can no more.

5. This also shall be sung in open places, as heaths, mountains, woods, and by streams and upon islands.

6. Moreover, ye shall build you fortified places in great cities, caverns and tombs shall be made glad with your praise.

7. Amen.

THE TREASURE HOUSE OF IMAGES

☀

Here beginneth the Book of
the Meditations on the
Twelvefold Adora-
tion, and the
Unity of
GOD.

The Chapter known as
The Perception of God
that is revealed unto man for a snare.

❖	❖	❖	❖	❖	**I**	❖	❖	❖	❖	❖
❖	❖	❖	❖		**adore**		❖	❖	❖	❖
❖	❖	❖			**Thee by the**			❖	❖	❖
❖	❖				**Twelvefold Snare**				❖	❖
❖					**and by the Unity thereof.**					❖

000. In the Beginning there was Naught, and Naught spake unto Naught saying: Let us beget on the Nakedness of our Nothingness the Limitless, Eternal, Identical, and United: And without will, intention, thought, word, desire, or deed, it was so.

00. Then in the depths of Nothingness hovered the Limitless, as a raven in the night; seeing naught, hearing naught, and understanding naught; neither was it seen, nor heard, nor understood; for as yet Countenance beheld not Countenance.

0. And as the Limitless stretched forth its wings, an unextended unextendable Light became; colourless, formless, conditionless, effluent, naked, and essential, as a crystalline dew of creative effulgence; and fluttering as a dove betwixt Day and Night, it vibrated forth a lustral Crown of Glory.

1. And out of the blinding whiteness of the Crown great an Eye, like unto an egg of an humming-bird cherished on a platter of burnished silver.

2. Thus I beheld Thee, O my God, the lid of whose Eye is as the Night of Chaos, and the pupil thereof as the marshalled order of the spheres.

3. For, I am but as a blind man, who wandering through the noontide perceiveth not the loveliness of day; and even as he whose eyes are unenlightened beholdeth not the greatness of this world in the depths of a starless night, so am I who am not able to search the unfathomable depths of Thy Wisdom.

4. For what am I that I durst look upon Thy Countenance, purblind one of small understanding that I am, blindly groping through the night

of mine ignorance like unto a little maggot hid in the dark depths of a corrupted corpse?

5. Therefore, O my God, fashion me into a five-pointed star of ruby burning beneath the foundations of Thy Unity, that I may mount the pillar of Thy Glory, and be lost in adoration of the triple Unity of Thy Godhead, I beseech Thee, O Thou who art to me as the Finger of Light thrust through the black clouds of Chaos; I beseech Thee, O my God, hearken Thou unto my cry!

6. Then, O my God, am I not risen as the sun that eateth up ocean as a golden lion that feedeth on a blue-grey wolf? So shall I become one with Thy Beauty, worn upon Thy breast as the Centre of a Sixfold Star of ruby and of sapphire.

7. Yea, O God, gird Thou me upon Thy thigh as a warrior girdeth his sword! Smite my acuteness into the earth, and as a sower casteth his seed into the furrows of the plough, do Thou beget upon me these adorations of Thy Unity, O My Conqueror!

8. And Thou shalt carry me upon Thine hip, O Thou flashing God, as a black mother of the South Country carrieth her babe. Whence I shall reach my lips so Thy pap, and sucking out Thy stars, shed them in these adorations upon the Earth.

9. Moreover, O God my God, Thou who hast cloven me with Thine amethystine Phallus, with Thy Phallus adamantine, with Thy Phallus of Gold and Ivory! thus am I cleft in twain as two halves of a child that is split asunder by the sword of the eunuchs, and mine adorations are divided, and one contendeth against his brother. Unite Thou me even as a split tree that closeth itself again upon the axe, that my song of praise unto Thee may be One Song!

10. For I am Thy chosen Virgin, O my God! Exalt Thou me unto the throne of the Mother, unto the Garden of Supernal Dew, unto the Unutterable Sea!

Amen,
and Amen of Amen,
and Amen of Amen of Amen,
and Amen of Amen of Amen of Amen.

♈ The Chapter known as
The Twelvefold Affirmations of God
and the Unity thereof

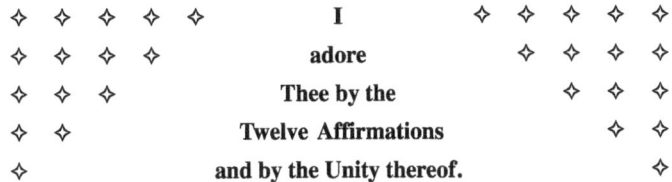

                I
            adore
         Thee by the
      Twelve Affirmations
    and by the Unity thereof.

1. O Thou snow-clad volcan of scarlet fire, Thou flamecrested pillar of fury! Yea, as I approach Thee, Thou departest from me like unto a wisp of smoke blown forth from the window of my house.

2. O Thou summer-land of eternal joy, Thou rapturous garden of flowers! Yea, as I gather Thee, my harvest is but as a drop of dew shimmering in the golden cup of the crocus.

3. O Thou throbbing music of life and death, Thou rhythmic harmony of the world! Yea, as I listen to the echo of Thy voice, my rapture is but as the whisper of the wings of a butterfly.

4. O Thou burning tempest of blinding sand, Thou whirlwind from the depths of darkness! yea, as I struggle through Thee, through Thee, my strength is but as a dove's down floating forth on the purple nipples of the storm.

5. O Thou crowned giant among great giants, Thou crimson-sworded soldier of war! Yea, as I battle with Thee, Thou masterest me as a lion that slayeth a babe that is cradled in lilies.

6. O Thou shadowy vista of Darkness, Thou cryptic Book of the firclad hills! Yea, as I search the key of Thy house I find my hope but as a rushlight sheltered in the hands of a little child.

7. O Thou great labour of the Firmament, Thou tempest-tossed roaring of the Aires! Yea, as I sink in the depths of Thine affliction, mine anguish is but as the smile on the lips of a sleeping babe.

8. O Thou depths of the Inconceivable, Thou cryptic, unutterable God! Yea, as I attempt to understand Thee, my wisdom is but as an abacus in the lap of an aged man.

9. O Thou tranfigured dream of blinding light, Thou beatitude of wonderment! Yea, as I behold Thee, mine understanding is but as the glimpse of a rainbow through a storm of blinding snow.

10. O Thou steel-girded mountain of mountains, Thou crested summit of Majesty! Yea, as I climb Thy grandeur, I find I have but surmounted one mote of dust floating in a beam of Thy Glory.

11. O Thou Empress of Light and of Darkness, Thou pourer-forth of the stars of night! Yea, as I gaze upon Thy Countenance, mine eyes are as the eyes of a blind man smitten by a torch of burning fire.

12. O Thou crimson gladness of the midnight, Thou flamingo North of brooding light! Yea, as I rise up before Thee, my joy is but as a raindrop smitten through by an arrow of the Western Sun.

13. O Thou golden Crown of the Universe, Thou diadem of dazzling brightness! Yea, as I burn up before Thee, my light is but as a falling star seen between the purple fingers of the Night.

> O Glory be unto Thee through all Time
> and through all Space: Glory,
> and Glory upon Glory
> Everlastingly. Amen,
> and Amen, and
> Amen.

The Chapter known as
The Twelvefold Renunciation of God
and the Unity thereof

❖ ❖ ❖ ❖ ❖   **I**   ❖ ❖ ❖ ❖ ❖
❖ ❖ ❖ ❖   **adore**   ❖ ❖ ❖ ❖
❖ ❖ ❖   **Thee by the**   ❖ ❖ ❖
❖ ❖   **Twelve Renunciations**   ❖ ❖
❖   **and by the Unity thereof.**   ❖

1. O my God, Thou mighty One, Thou Creator of all things, I renounce unto Thee the kisses of my mistress, and the murmur of her mouth, and all the trembling of her firm young breast; so that I may be rolled a flame in Thy fiery embrace, and be consumed in the unutterable joy of Thine everlasting rapture.

2. O my God, Thou mighty One, Thou Creator of all things, I renounce unto Thee the soft-lipp'd joys of life, and the honey-sweets of this world, and all the subtilities of the flesh; so that I may be feasted on the fire of Thy passion, and be consumed in the unutterable joy of Thine everlasting rapture.

3. O my God, Thou Mighty One, Thou Creator of all things, I renounce unto Thee the ceaseless booming of the waves, and the fury of the storm, and all the turmoil of the wind-swept waters; so that I may drink of the porphyrine foam of Thy lips, and be consumed in the unutterable joy of Thine everlasting rapture.

4. O my God, Thou Mighty One, Thou Creator of all things, I renounce unto Thee the whispers of the desert, and the moan of the simoom, and all the silence of the sea of dust; so that I may be lost in the atoms of Thy Glory, and be consumed in the unutterable joy of Thine everlasting rapture.

5. O my God, Thou Mighty One, Thou Creator of all things, I renounce unto Thee the green fields of the valleys, and the satyr roses of the hills, and the nymph lilies of the meer; so that I may wander through the

gardens of Thy Splendor, and be consumed in the unutterable joy of Thine everlasting rapture.

6. O my God, Thou Mighty One, Thou Creator of all things, I renounce unto Thee the sorrow of my mother, and the threshold of my home, and all the labour of my father's hands; so that I may be led unto the Mansion of Thy Light, and be consumed in the unutterable joy of Thine everlasting rapture.

7. O my God, Thou Mighty One, Thou Creator of all things, I renounce unto Thee the yearning for Paradise, and the dark fear of Hell, and the feast of the corruption of the grave; so that as a child I may be led unto Thy Kingdom, and be consumed in the unutterable joy of Thine everlasting rapture.

8. O my God, Thou Mighty One, Thou Creator of all things, I renounce unto Thee the moonlit peaks of the mountains, and the arrow-shapen kiss of the firs, and all the travail of the winds, so that I may be lost on the summit of Thy Glory, and be consumed in the unutterable joy of Thine everlasting rapture.

9. O my God, Thou Mighty One, Thou Creator of all things, I renounce unto Thee the goatish ache of the years, and the cryptic books, and all the majesty of their enshrouded words; so that I may be entangled in Thy wordless Wisdom, and be consumed in the unutterable joy of Thine everlasting rapture.

10. O my God, Thou Mighty One, Thou Creator of all things, I renounce unto Thee the wine-cups of merriment, and the eyes of the wanton bearers, and all the lure of their soft limbs, so that I may be made drunk on the vine of Thy splendour, and be consumed in the unutterable joy of Thine everlasting rapture.

11. O my God, Thou Mighty One, Thou Creator of all things, I renounce unto Thee the hissing of mad waters, and the trumpeting of the thunder, and all Thy tongues of dancing flames, so that I may be swept up in the breath of Thy nostrils, and be consumed in the unutterable joy of Thine everlasting rapture.

12. O my God, Thou Mighty One, Thou Creator of all things, I renounce unto Thee the crimson lust of the chase, and the blast of the brazen war-horns, and all the gleaming of the spears; so that like an hart I may be brought to bay in Thine arms, and be consumed in the unutterable joy of Thine everlasting rapture.

13. O my God, Thou Mighty One, Thou Creator of all things, I renounce unto Thee all that Self which is myself, that black sun which shineth in Self's day, whose glory blindeth Thy Glory; so that I may become as a rushlight in Thine abode, and be consumed in the unutterable joy of Thine everlasting rapture.

> O Glory be unto Thee through all Time
> and through all Space: Glory,
> and Glory upon Glory
> Everlastingly. Amen,
> and Amen, and
> Amen.

II. The Chapter known as The Twelvefold Conjuration of God and the Unity thereof

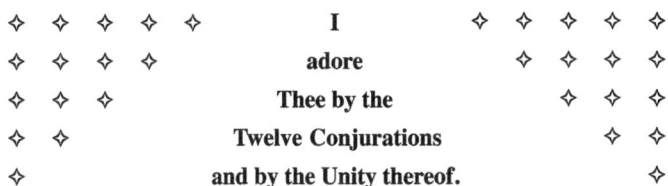

1. O Thou Consuming Eye of everlasting light set as a pearl betwixt the lids of Night and Day; I swear to Thee by the formless void of the Abyss, to lap the galaxies of night in darkness, and blow the meteors like bubbles into the frothing jaws of the sun.

2. O Thou ten-footed soldier of blue ocean, whose castle is built upon the sands of life and death; I swear to Thee by the glittering blades of the waters, to cleave my way within Thine armed hermitage, and brood as an eyeless corpse beneath the coffin-lid of the Mighty Sea.

3. O thou incandescent Ocean of molten stars, surging above the arch of the Firmament; I swear to Thee by the mane-pennoned lances of light, to stir the lion of Thy darkness from its lair, and lash the sorceress of noon-tide into fury with serpents of fire.

4. O Thou intoxicating Vision of Beauty, fair as ten jewelled virgins dancing about the hermit moon; I swear to Thee by the peridot flagons of spring, to quaff to the dregs Thy chalice of Glory, and beget a royal race before the Dawn flees from awakening Day.

5. O Thou unalterable measure of all things, in whose lap lie the destinies of unborn worlds; I swear to Thee by the balance of Light and Darkness, to spread out the blue vault as a looking-glass, and flash forth therefrom the intolerable lustre of Thy Countenance.

6. O Thou who settest forth the limitless expanse, spanned by wings of thunder above the cosmic strife; I swear to Thee by the voiceless dust of the desert, to soar above the echos of shreiking life, and as an eagle to feast for ever upon the silence of the stars.

7. O Thou flame-tipped arrow of devouring fire that quiverest as a tongue in the dark mouth of Night; I swear to Thee by the thurible of Thy Glory, to breathe the incense of mine understanding, and to cast the ashes of my wisdom into the Valley of Thy breast.

8. O Thou ruin of the mountains, glistening as an old white wolf above the fleecy mists of Earth; I swear to Thee by the galaxies of Thy domain, to press Thy lamb's breasts with the teeth of my soul, and drink of the milk and blood of Thy subtlety and innocence.

9. O Thou Eternal river of chaotic law, in whose depths lie locked the secrets of Creation; I swear to Thee by the primal waters of the Deep, to suck up the Firmament of Thy Chaos, and as a volcano to belch forth a Cosmos of coruscating suns.

10. O Thou Dragon-regent of the blue sea of air, as a chain of emeralds round the neck of Space, I swear to Thee by the hexagram of Night and Day, to be unto Thee as the twin fish of Time, which being set apart never divulge the secret of their unity.

11. O Thou flame of horned storm-clouds, that sunderest their desolation, that outroarest the winds, I swear to Thee by the gleaming sandals of the stars, to climb beyond the summits of the mountains, and rend Thy robe of purple thunders with a sword of silvery light.

12. O Thou fat of an hundred fortresses of iron, crimson as the blades of a million murderous swords; I swear to Thee by the smoke-wreath of the volcano, to open the secret shrine of Thy bull's breast, and tear out as an auger the heart of Thine all-pervading mystery.

13. O Thou silver axle of the Wheel of Being, thrust through the wings of Time by the still hand of Space; I swear to Thee by the twelve spokes of Thy Unity, to become unto Thee as the rim thereof, so that I may clothe me majestically in the robe that has no seam.

O Glory be unto Thee through all Time
and through all Space: Glory,
and Glory upon Glory
Everlastingly. Amen,
and Amen, and
Amen.

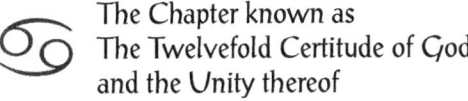

The Chapter known as
The Twelvefold Certitude of God
and the Unity thereof

   ✧ ✧ ✧ ✧ ✧   **I**   ✧ ✧ ✧ ✧ ✧
   ✧ ✧ ✧ ✧   **adore**   ✧ ✧ ✧ ✧
   ✧ ✧ ✧   **Thee by the**   ✧ ✧ ✧
   ✧ ✧   **Twelve Certitudes**   ✧ ✧
   ✧   **and by the Unity thereof.**   ✧

1. O Thou Sovran Warrior of steel-girt valour, whose scimitar is a flame between day and night, whose helm is crested with the wings of the Abyss. I know thee! O Thou four-eyed guardian of heaven, who kindleth to a flame the hearts of the downcast, and girdeth about with fire the loins of the unarmed.

2. O Thou Sovran Light and fire of loveliness, whose flaming locks stream downwards through the æthyr as knots of lightening deep-rooted in the Abyss. I know thee! O Thou winnowing flail of brightness, the passionate lash of whose encircling hand scatters mankind before Thy fury as the wind-scud from the stormy breast of the Ocean.

3. O Thou Sovran Singer of the revelling winds, whose voice is as a vestal troop of Bacchanals awakened by the piping of a Pan-pipe. I know thee! O Thou dancing flame of frenzied song, whose shouts, like unto golden swords of leaping fire, urge us onward to the wild slaughter of the Worlds.

4. O Thou Sovran Might of the most ancient forests, whose voice is as the murmur of unappeasable winds caught up in the arms of the swaying branches. I know Thee! O Thou rumble of conquering drums, who lulleth to a rapture of deep sleep those lovers who burn into each other, flame to fine flame.

5. O Thou Sovran Guide of the star-wheeling circles, the soles of whose feet smite plumes of golden fire from the outermost annihilation of the Abyss. I know Thee! O Thou crimson sword of destruction, whose chasest the comets from the dark bed of night, till they speed before Thee as serpent tongues of flame.

6. O Thou Sovran Archer of the darksome regions, who shooteth forth from Thy transcendental crossbow the many-rayed suns into the fields of heave. I know Thee! O Thou eight-pointed arrow of light, who smiteth the regions of the seven rivers until they laugh like Mænads with snaky thyrsus.

7. O Thou Sovran Paladin of self-vanquished knights, whose path lieth through the trackless forest of time, winding athrough the Byss of unbegotten space. I know Thee! O Thou despiser of the mountains, Thou whose course is as that of a lightening-hoofed steed leaping along the green bank of a fair river.

8. O Thou Sovran Surging of wild felicity, whose love is as the overflowing of the seas, and who makest our bodies to laugh with beauty. I know Thee! O Thou outstrider of the sunset, who deckest the snow-capped mountains with red roses, and strewest white violets on the curling waves.

9. O Thou Sovran Diadem of crowned Wisdom, whose work knoweth the path of the sylphs of the air, and the black burrowings of the gnomes of the earth. I know Thee! O Thou Master of the ways of life, in the palm of whose hand all the arts lie bounden as a smoke-cloud betwixt thy lips of the mountain.

10. O Thou Sovran Lord of primæval Baresarkers, who huntest with dawn the dappled deer of twilight, and whose engines of war are blood-crested comets. I know Thee! O Thou flame-crowned Self-luminous One, the lash of whose whip gathered the ancient worlds, and looseth the blood from the virgin clouds of heaven.

11. O Thou Sovran Moonstone of pearly loveliness, from out whose many eyes flash the fire-clouds of life, and whose breath enkindleth the

Bliss and the Abyss. I know Thee! O Thou fountain-head of fierce æthyr, in the pupil of whose brightness all things lie crouched and wrapped like a babe in the womb of its mother.

12. O Thou Sovran Mother of the breath of being, the milk of whose breasts is as the fountain of love, twin-jets of fire upon the blue bosom of night. I know Thee! O Thou Virgin of the moonlit glades, who fondleth us as a drop of dew in Thy lap, ever watchful over the cradle of our fate.

13. O Thou Sovran All-Beholding eternal Sun, who lappest up the constellations of heave, as a thirsty thief of jar of ancient wine. I know Thee! O Thou dawn-wind'd courtesan of light, who makest me to reel with one kiss of Thy mouth, as a leaf cast into the flames of a furnace.

O Glory be unto Thee through all Time
and through all Space: Glory,
and Glory upon Glory
Everlastingly. Amen,
and Amen, and
Amen.

The Chapter known as
The Twelvefold Glorification of God
and the Unity thereof

    ✧ ✧ ✧ ✧ ✧   **I**   ✧ ✧ ✧ ✧ ✧

    ✧ ✧ ✧ ✧   **adore**   ✧ ✧ ✧ ✧

    ✧ ✧ ✧   **Thee by the**   ✧ ✧ ✧

    ✧ ✧   **Twelve Glorifications**   ✧ ✧

    ✧   **and by the Unity thereof.**   ✧

1. O Glory be to Thee, O God of my God; for I behold Thee in the Lion Rampant of the dawn; Thou hast crushed with Thy paw the crouching lioness of Night; so that she may roar forth the Glory of Thy Name.

2. O Glory be to Thee, O God of my God; for I behold Thee in the lap of the fertile valleys; Thou hast adorned their strong limbs with a robe of poppied corn, so that they may laugh forth the Glory of Thy Name.

3. O Glory be to Thee, O God of my God; for I behold Thee in the gilded rout of dancing-girls: Thou hast garlanded their naked middles with fragrant flowers, so that they may pace forth the Glory of Thy Name.

4. O Glory be to Thee, O God of my God; for I behold Thee in the riotous joy of the storm: Thou hast shaken the gold-dust from the tresses of the hills, so that they may chaunt forth the Glory of Thy Name.

5. O Glory be to Thee, O God of my God; for I behold Thee in the stars and meteors of Night: Thou hast caparisoned her grey coursers with moons of pearl, so that hey may shake forth the Glory of Thy Name.

6. O Glory be to Thee, O God of my God; for I behold Thee in the precious stones of the black earth: Thou hast lightened her with a myriad eyes of magic, so that she may wink forth the Glory of Thy Name.

7. O Glory be to Thee, O God of my God; for I behold Thee in the sparkling dew of the wild glades: Thou hast decked them out as for a great feast of rejoicing, so that they may gleam forth the Glory of Thy Name.

8. O Glory be to Thee, O God of my God; for I behold Thee in the

stillness of the frozen lakes: Thou hast made their faces more dazzling than a silver mirror, so that they may flash forth the Glory of Thy Name.

9. O Glory be to Thee, O God of my God; for I behold Thee in the smoke-veil'd fire of the mountains: Thou hast inflamed them as lions that scent a fallow deer, so that they may rage forth the Glory of Thy Name.

10. O Glory be to Thee, O God of my God; for I behold Thee in the countenance of my darling: Thou hast unclothed her of white lilies and crimson roses, so that she may blush forth the Glory of Thy Name.

11. O Glory be to Thee, O God of my God; for I behold Thee in the weeping of the flying clouds: Thou hast swelled therewith the blue breasts of the milky rivers, so that they may roll forth the Glory of Thy Name.

12. O Glory be to Thee, O God of my God; for I behold Thee in the amber combers of the storm: Thou hast laid Thy lash upon the sphinxes of the waters, so that they may boom forth the Glory of Thy Name.

13. O Glory be to Thee, O God of my God; for I behold Thee in the lotus-flower within my heart: Thou hast emblazoned my trumpet with the lion-standard, so that I may blare forth the Glory of Thy Name.

> O Glory be unto Thee through all Time
> and through all Space: Glory,
> and Glory upon Glory
> Everlastingly. Amen,
> and Amen, and
> Amen.

♍ The Chapter known as The Twelvefold Beseechment of God and the Unity thereof

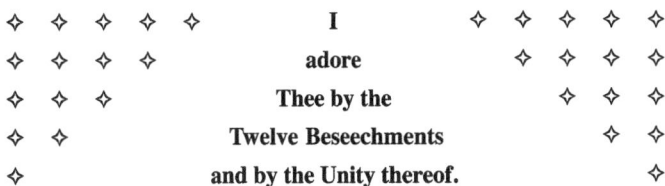

1. O Thou mighty God, make me as a fair virgin that is clad in the blue-bells of the fragrant hillside; I beseech Thee, O Thou great God! That I may ring out the melody of Thy voice and be clothed in the pure light of Thy loveliness: O Thou God my God!

2. O Thou mighty God, make me as a Balance of rubies and jet that is cast in the lap of the Sun; I beseech Thee, O Thou great God! That I may flash forth the wonder of Thy brightness, and melt into the perfect poise of Thy Being: O Thou God my God!

3. O Thou mighty God, make me as a brown Scorpion that creepeth on through a vast desert of silver; I beseech Thee, O Thou great God! That I lose myself in the span of Thy light, and become one with the glitter of Thy Shadow: O Thou God my God!

4. O Thou mighty God, make me as a green arrow of Lightning that speedeth through the purple clouds of Night; I beseech Thee, O Thou great God! That I may wake fire from the crown of Thy Wisdom, and flash into the depths of Thine Understanding: O Thou God my God!

5. O Thou mighty God, make me as a flint-black goat that pranceth in a shining wilderness of steel; I beseech Thee, O Thou great God! That I may paw one flashing spark from Thy Splendour, and be welded into the Glory of Thy might: O Thou God my God!

6. O Thou mighty God, make me as the sapphirine waves that cling to the shimmering limbs of the green rocks; I beseech Thee, O Thou great God! That I may chant in foaming music Thy Glory, and roll forth the eternal rapture of Thy Name: O Thou God my God!

7. O Thou mighty God, make me as a silver fish darting through the vast depths of the dim-peopled waters; I beseech Thee, O Thou great God! That I may swim through the vastness of Thine abyss, and sink beneath the waveless depths of Thy Glory: O Thou God my God!

8. O Thou mighty God, make me as a white ram that is athirst in a sun-scorched desert of bitterness; I beseech Thee, O Thou great God! That I may seek the deep waters of Thy Wisdom, and plunge into the whiteness of Thine effulgence: O Thou God my God!

9. O Thou mighty God, make me as a thunder-smitten bull that is drunk upon the vintage of Thy blood; I beseech Thee, O Thou great God! That I may bellow through the universe Thy Power, and trample the nectar-sweet grapes of Thine Essence: O Thou God my God!

10. O Thou mighty God, make me as a black eunuch of song that is twin-voiced, yet dumb in either tongue; I beseech Thee, O Thou great God! That I may hush my melody in Thy Silence, and swell into the sweet ecstasy of Thy Song. O Thou God my God!

11. O Thou mighty God, make me as an emerald crab that crawleth over the wet sands of the sea-shore; I beseech Thee, O Thou great God! That I may write Thy name across the shores of Time, and sink amongst the white atoms of Thy Being. O Thou God my God!

12. O Thou mighty God, make me as a ruby lion that roareth from the summit of a white mountain; I beseech Thee, O Thou great God! That I may echo forth Thy lordship through the hills, and dwindle into the nipple of Thy bounty. O Thou God my God!

13. O Thou mighty God, make me as an all-consuming Sun ablaze in the centre of the Universe; I beseech Thee, O Thou great God! That I may become as a crown upon Thy brow, and flash forth the exceeding fire of Thy Godhead: O Thou God my God!

> O Glory be unto Thee through all Time
> and through all Space: Glory,
> and Glory upon Glory
> Everlastingly. Amen,
> and Amen, and
> Amen.

The Chapter known as The Twelvefold Gratification of God and the Unity thereof

              I
           adore
        Thee by the
     Twelve Gratifications
and by the Unity thereof.

1. O Thou green-cloaked Mænad in labour, who bearest beneath Thy leaden girdle the vintage of Thy kisses; release me from the darkness of Thy womb, so that I may cast off my infant wrappings and leap forth as an armed warrior in steel.

2. O Thou snake of misty countenance, whose braided hair is like a fleecy dawn of swooning maidens; hunt me as a fierce wild boar through the skies, so that Thy burning spear may gore the blue heavens red with the foaming blood of my frenzy.

3. O Thou cloudy Virgin of the World, whose breasts are as scarlet lilies paling before the sun; dandle me in the cradle of Thine arms, so that the murmur of Thy voice may lull me to a sleep like a pearl lost in the depths of a silent sea.

4. O Thou wine-voiced laughter of fainting gloom, who art as a naked faun crushed to death between millstones of thunder; make me drunk on the rapture of Thy song, so that in the corpse-clutch of my passion I may tear the cloud-robe from off Thy swooning breast.

5. O Thou wanton cup-bearer of madness, whose mouth is as the joy of a thousand masterful kisses; intoxicate me on Thy loveliness, so that the silver of Thy merriment may revel as a moon-white pearl upon my tongue.

6. O Thou midnight Vision of Whiteness, whose lips are as pouting rosebuds deflowered by the deciduous moon; tend me as a drop of dew in Thy breast, so that the dragon of Thy gluttonous hate may devour me with its mouth of adamant.

7. O Thou effulgence of burning love, who pursueth the dawn as a youth pursueth a rose-lipped maiden; rend me with the fierce kisses of Thy mouth, so that in the battle of our lips I may be drenched by the snow-pure fountains of Thy bliss.

8. O Thou black bull in field of white girls, whose foaming flanks are as starry night ravished in the fierce arms of noon; shake forth the purple horns of my passion, so that I may dissolve as a crown of fire in the bewilderment of Thine ecstasy.

9. O Thou dread arbiter of all men, the hem of whose broidered skirt crimsoneth the white battlements of Space; bare me the starry nipple of Thy breast, so that the milk of Thy love may nurture me to the lustiness of Thy virginity.

10. O Thou thirsty charioteer of Time, whose cup is the hollow night filled with the foam of the vintage of day; drench me in the shower of Thy passion, so that I may pant in Thine arms as a tongue of lightning on the purple bosom of night.

11. O Thou opalescent Serpent-Queen, whose mouth is as the sunset that is bloody with the slaughter of day; hold me in the crimson flames of Thine arms, so that at Thy kisses I may expire as a bubble in the foam of Thy dazzling lips.

12. O Thou Odalisque of earth's palace, whose garments are scented and passionate as spring flowers in sunlit glades; roll me in the sweet perfume of Thy hair, so that Thy tresses of gold may anoint me with the honey of a million roses.

13. O Thou manly warrior amongst youths, whose limbs are as swords of fire that are welded in the furnaces of war; press Thy cool kisses to my burning lips, so that the folly of our passion may weave us into the Crown of everlasting Light.

> O Glory be unto Thee through all Time
> and through all Space: Glory,
> and Glory upon Glory
> Everlastingly. Amen,
> and Amen, and
> Amen.

♏ The Chapter known as
The Twelvefold Denial of God
and the Unity thereof

✧	✧	✧	✧	✧	**I**	✧	✧	✧	✧	✧
	✧	✧	✧	✧	**adore**		✧	✧	✧	✧
		✧	✧	✧	**Thee by the**			✧	✧	✧
			✧	✧	**Twelve Denials**				✧	✧
				✧	**and by the Unity thereof.**					✧

1. O Thou God of the Nothingness of All Things! Thou who art neither the Formless breath of Chaos; nor the exhaler of the ordered spheres:

O Thou who art not the cloud-cradled star of the morning; nor the sun, drunken upon the mist, who blindeth men!

I deny Thee by the powers of mine understanding;

Guide me in the unity of Thy might, and lead me to the fatherhood of Thine all-pervading Nothingness'

for Thou art all and none of these in the fullness of Thy Not-Being.

2. O Thou God of Nothingness of All Things!

Thou who art neither the vitality of worlds; nor the breath of star-entangled Being:

O Thou who art not horsed 'mid the centaur clouds of night; nor the twanging of the shuddering bowstring of noon!

I deny Thee by the powers of mind understanding;

Throne me in the unity of Thy might, and stab me with the javelin of Thine all-pervading Nothingness;

for Thou art all and none of these in the fullness of Thy Not-Being.

3. O Thou God of the Nothingness of All Things!

Thou who art neither the Pan-pipe in the forest; nor life's blue sword wrapped in the cloak of death:

O Thou who art not found amongst the echoes of the hills; nor in the whisperings that wake with the valleys!

I deny Thee by the powers of mind understanding;

Crown me in the unity of Thy might, and flash me as a scarlet tongue into Thine all-pervading Nothingness'

for Thou art all and none of these in the fullness of Thy Not-Being.

4. O Thou God of the Nothingness of All Things!

Thou who art neither the Crown of the flaming storm; nor the opalescence of the Abyss:

O Thou who art not a nymph in the foam of the sea; nor a whirling devil in the sand of the desert!

I deny Thee by the powers of mine understanding.

Bear me in the unity of Thy might, and pour me forth from out the cup of Thine all-pervading Nothingness;

for Thou art all and none of these in the fullness of Thy Not-Being

5. O Thou God of the Nothingness of All Things!

Thou who art neither the formulator of law; nor the Cheat of the maze of illusion:

O Thou who art not the foundation-stone of existence; nor the eagle that broodeth upon the egg of space!

I deny Thee by the powers of mine understanding;

Swathe me in the unity of Thy might, and teach me wisdom from the lips of Thine all-pervading Nothingness;

for Thou art all and none of these in the fullness of Thy Not-Being

6. O Thou God of the Nothingness of All Things!

Thou who art neither the fivefold root of Nature; nor the fire-crested helm of her Master:

O Thou who art not the Emperor of Eternal Time; nor the warrior shout that rocketh the Byss of Space!

I deny Thee by the powers of mine understanding;

Raise me in the unity of Thy might, and suckle me at the swol'n breasts of Thine all pervading-Nothingness;

for Thou art all and none of these in the fullness of Thy Not-Being

7. O Thou God of the Nothingness of All Things!

Thou who art neither the golden bull of the heavens; nor the crimsoned fountain of the lusts of men:

O Thou who reclinest not upon the Waggon of Night; nor restest Thine hand upon the handle of the Plough!

I deny Thee by the powers of mine understanding;

Urge me in the unity of Thy might, and drench me with the red vintage of Thine all-pervading Nothingness;

for Thou art all and none of these in the fullness of Thy Not-Being

8. O Thou God of the Nothingness of All Things!

Thou who art neither the starry eyes of heavens; nor the forehead of the crownèd morning;

O Thou who art not perceived by the powers of the mind; nor grasped by the fingers of Silence or of Speech!

I deny Thee by the powers of mine understanding;

Robe me in the unity of Thy might, and speed me into the blindness of Thine all-pervading Nothingness;

for Thou art all and none of these in the fullness of Thy Not-Being

9. O Thou God of the Nothingness of All Things!

Thou who art neither the forge in the hissing of the hail-stones; nor in the rioting of the equinoctial storm!

I deny Thee by the powers of mine understanding;

Bring me to the unity of Thy might, and feast me on honeyed manna of Thine all-pervading Nothingness;

for Thou art all and none of these in the fullness of Thy Not-Being

10. O Thou God of the Nothingness of All Things!

Thou who art neither the traces of the chariot; nor the pole of galloping delusion:

O Thou who art not the pivot of the whole Universe; nor the body of the woman-serpent of the stars!

I deny Thee by the powers of mine understanding;

Lead me in the unity of Thy might, and draw me unto the threshold of Thine of Thine all-pervading Nothingness;

for Thou art all and none of these in the fullness of Thy Not-Being

11. O Thou God of the Nothingness of All Things!

Thou who art neither the moaning of a maiden; nor the electric touch of fire-thrilled youth:

O thou who art not found in the hardy kisses of love; nor in the tortured spasms of madness and of hate!

I deny Thee by the powers of mine understanding;

Weight me in the unity of Thy might, and roll me in the poised rapture of Thine all-pervading Nothingness;

for Thou art all and none of these in the fullness of Thy Not-Being

12. O Thou God of the Nothingness of All Things!

Thou who art neither the primal cause of causes; nor the soul of what is, or was, or will be:

O Thou who art not measured in the motionless balance; nor smitten by the arrow-flights of man!

I deny Thee by the powers of mine understanding;

Shield me in the unity of Thy might, and reckon me aright in the span of Thine all-pervading Nothingness;

for Thou art all and none of these in the fullness of Thy Not-Being

13. O Thou God of the Nothingness of All Things!

Thou who art neither the breathing influx of life; nor the iron ring i' the marriage feast of death:

O Thou who art not shadowed forth in the songs of war; nor in the tears or lamentations of a child!

I deny Thee by the powers of mine understanding;

Sheathe me in the unity of Thy might, and kindle me with the grey flame of Thine all-pervading Nothingness:

for Thou art all and none of these in the fullness of Thy Not-Being

> O Glory be unto Thee through all Time
> and through all Space: Glory,
> and Glory upon Glory
> Everlastingly. Amen,
> and Amen, and
> Amen.

The Chapter known as The Twelvefold Rejoicing of God and the Unity thereof

❖ ❖ ❖ ❖ ❖   **I**   ❖ ❖ ❖ ❖ ❖
❖ ❖ ❖ ❖   **adore**   ❖ ❖ ❖ ❖
❖ ❖ ❖   **Thee by the**   ❖ ❖ ❖
❖ ❖   **Twelve Rejoicings**   ❖ ❖
❖   **and by the Unity thereof.**   ❖

1. Ah! but I rejoice in Thee, O Thou my God;
Thou seven-rayed rainbow of perfect loveliness;
Thou light-rolling chariot of sunbeams;
Thou fragrant scent of the passing storm:
Yea, I rejoice in Thee, Thou breath of the slumbering valleys;
O Thou low-murmuring ripple of the ripe cornfields!

I rejoice, yea, I shout in gladness! till, as the mingling blushes of day and night, my song weaveth the joys of life into a gold and purple Crown, for the Glory of Splendour of Thy Name.

2. Ah! but I rejoice in Thee, O Thou my God;
Thou zigzagged effulgence of the burning stars;
Thou wilderment of indigo light;
Thou grey horn of immaculate fire:

Yea, I rejoice in Thee, Thou embattled cloud of flashing flame;

O Thou capricious serpent-head of scarlet hair!

I rejoice, yea, I shout with gladness! till my roaring filleth the wooded mountains, and like a giant forceth the wind's head through the struggling trees, in the Glory and Splendour of Thy Name.

3. Ah! but I rejoice in Thee, O Thou my God;

Thou silken web of emerald bewitchment;

Thou berylline mist of marshy meers;

Thou flame-spangled fleece of seething gold:

Yea, I rejoice in Thee, Thou pearly dew of the setting moon;

O Thou dark purple storm-cloud of contending kisses!

I rejoice, yea, I shout with gladness! till all my laughter, like enchanted waters, is blown as an iris-web of bubbles from the lips of the deep, in the Glory of Splendour of Thy Name.

4. Ah! but I rejoice in Thee, O Thou my God;

Thou who broodest on the dark depths of the deep;

Thou lap of the wave-glittering sea;

Thou bright vesture of the crested floods:

Yea, I rejoice in Thee, Thou native splendour of the Waters;

O Thou fathomless Abyss of surging joy!

I rejoice, yea, I shout with gladness! till the mad swords of my music smite the hills, and rend the amethyst limbs of Night from the white embrace of Day, at the Glory of Splendour of Thy Name.

5. Ah! but I rejoice in Thee, O Thou my God;

Thou cloud-hooded bastion of the stormy skies;

Thou lightning anvil of angel swords;

Thou gloomy forge of the thunderbold:

Yea, I rejoice in Thee, Thou all-subduing Crown of Splendour;

O Thou hero-souled helm of endless victory!

I rejoice, yea, I shout with gladness! till the mad rivers rush roaring through the woods, and my re-echoing voice danceth like a ram among the hills, for the Glory of Splendour of Thy Name.

6. Ah! but I rejoice in Thee, O Thou my God;

Thou opalescent orb of shattered sunsets;

Thou pearly boss on the shield of light; Thou tawny priest at the Mass of lust:

Yea, I rejoice in Thee, Thou chalcedony cloudland of light:

O Thou poppy-petal floating upon the snowstorm!

I rejoice, yea, I shout with gladness! till my frenzied words rush through the souls of men, like a blood-red bull through a white heard of terror-stricken kine, at the Glory of Splendour of Thy Name.

7. Ah! but I rejoice in Thee, O Thou my God;

Thou unimperilled flight of joyous laughter;

Thou eunuch glaive-armed before joy's veil;

Thou dreadful insatiable One:

Yea, I rejoice in Thee, Thou lofty gathering-point of Bliss;

O Thou bridal-bed of murmuring rapture!

I rejoice, yea, I shout with gladness! till I tangle the black tresses of the storm, and last the tempest into a green foam of twining basilisks, in the Glory and Splendour of Thy Name.

8. Ah! but I rejoice in Thee, O Thou my God;

Thou coruscating star-point of Endlessness;

Thou inundating fire of the Void;

Thou moonbeam cup of eternal life:

Yea, I rejoice in Thee, Thou fire-sandalled warrior of steel:

O Thou bloody dew of the field of slaughter and death!

I rejoice, yea, I shout with gladness! till the music of my throat smiteth the hills as a crescent moon waketh a nightly field of sleeping comets, at the Glory of Splendour of Thy Name.

9. Ah! but I rejoice in Thee, O Thou my God;

Thou jewel-work of snow on the limbs of night;

Thou elaboration of oneness;

Thou shower of universal suns:

Yea, I rejoice in Thee, Thou gorgeous, Thou wildering one;

O Thou great lion roaring over a sea of blood!

I rejoice, yea, I shout with gladness! till the wild thunder of my praise breaketh down, as a satyr doth a babe, the nine and ninety gates of Thy Power, in the Glory of Splendour of Thy Name.

10. Ah! but I rejoice in Thee, O Thou my God;

Thou ambrosia-yielding rose of the World;

Thou vaulted dome of effulgent light;

Thou valley of venomous vipers;

Yea, I rejoice in Thee, Thou dazzling robe of the soft rain-clouds;

O Thou lion-voiced up-rearing of the goaded storm!

I rejoice, yea, I should with gladness! till my rapture, like unto a two-edged sword, traceth a sigil of fire and blasteth the banded sorcerers, in the Glory of Splendour of Thy Name.

11. Ah! but I rejoice in Thee, O Thou my God;

Thou Crown of unutterable loveliness;

Thou feather of hyalescent flame;

Thou all-beholding eye of brightness;

Yea, I rejoice in Thee, Thou resplendent everlasting one:

O Thou vast abysmal ocean of foaming flames!

I rejoice, yea, I shout with gladness! till the stars leap like white coursers from the night, and the heavens resound as an army of steel-clad warriors, at the Glory of Splendour of Thy Name.

12. Ah! but I rejoice in Thee, O Thou my God;

Thou star-blaze of undying expectation;

Thou ibis-throated voice of silence;

Thou blinding night of understanding:

Yea, I rejoice in Thee, Thou white finger of Chaotic law;

O Thou creative cockatrice twined amongst the waters!

I rejoice, yea, I shout with gladness! till my cries stir the night as the burnished gold a lance thrust into a poisonous dragon of adamant, for the Glory of Splendour of Thy Name.

13. Ah! but I rejoice in Thee, O Thou my God;
Thou self-luminous refulgent Brilliance;
Thou eye of light that hath no eyelid;
Thou turquoise-studded sceptre of deed:
Yea, I rejoice in Thee, Thou white furnace womb of Energy;
O Thou spark-whirling forge of the substance of the worlds;

I rejoice, yea, I shout with gladness! till I mount as a white beam unto the crown, and as a breath of night melt into the golden lips of Thy dawn, in the Glory of Splendour of Thy Name.

> O Glory be unto Thee through all Time
> and through all Space: Glory,
> and Glory upon Glory
> Everlastingly. Amen,
> and Amen, and
> Amen.

The Chapter known as The Twelvefold Humiliation of God and the Unity thereof

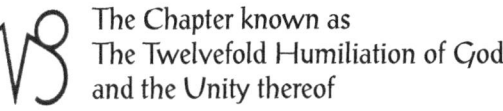

✧ ✧ ✧ ✧ ✧   **I**   ✧ ✧ ✧ ✧ ✧
✧ ✧ ✧ ✧   **adore**   ✧ ✧ ✧ ✧
✧ ✧ ✧   **Thee by the**   ✧ ✧ ✧
✧ ✧   **Twelve Humiliations**   ✧ ✧
✧   **and by the Unity thereof.**   ✧

1. O my God, behold me fully and be merciful unto me, as I humble myself before Thee; for all my searching is as a bat that seeks some hollow of night upon a sun-parched wilderness.

2. O my God, order me justly and be merciful unto me, as I humble myself before Thee; for all my thoughts are as a dust-clad serpent wind at noon that danceth through the ashen grass of law.

3. O my God, conquer me with love and be merciful unto me, as I humble myself before Thee; for all the striving of my spirit is as a child's kiss that struggles through a cloud of tangled hair.

4. O my God, suckle me with truth and be merciful unto me, as I humble myself before Thee; for all my agony of anguish is but as a quail struggling in the jaws of an hungry wolf.

5. O my God, comfort me with ease and be merciful unto me, as I humble myself before Thee; for all the toil of my life is but a small white mouse swimming through a vast sea of crimson blood

6. O my God, entreat me gently and be merciful unto me, as I humble myself before Thee; for all my toil is but as a threadless shuttle thrust here and there in the black loom of night.

7. O my God, fondle me with kisses and be merciful unto me, as I humble myself before Thee; for all my desires are as dewdrops that are sucked from silver lilies by the throat of a young god.

8. O my God, exalt me with blood and be merciful unto me, as I humble myself before Thee; for all my courage is but as the fang of a viper that striketh at the rosy heel of dawn.

9. O my God, teach me with patience and be merciful unto me, as I humble myself before Thee, for all my knowledge is but as the refuse of the chaff that is flung to the darkness of the void.

10. O my God, measure me rightly and be merciful unto me, as I humble myself before Thee; for all my praise is but a single letter of lead lost in the gilded scriptures of the rocks.

11. O my God, fill me with slumber and be merciful unto me, as I humble myself before Thee; for all my wakefulness is but as a cloud at sunset that is like a snake gliding through the dew.

12. O my God, kindle me with joy and be merciful unto me, as I humble myself before Thee; for all the strength of my mind is but as a web of silk that bindeth the milky breasts of the stars.

13. O my God, consume me with fire and be merciful unto me, as I humble myself before Thee; for all mine understanding is but a spider's thread drawn from star to star of a young galaxy.

> O Glory be unto Thee through all Time
> and through all Space: Glory,
> and Glory upon Glory
> Everlastingly. Amen,
> and Amen, and
> Amen.

The Chapter known as The Twelvefold Lamentation of God and the Unity thereof

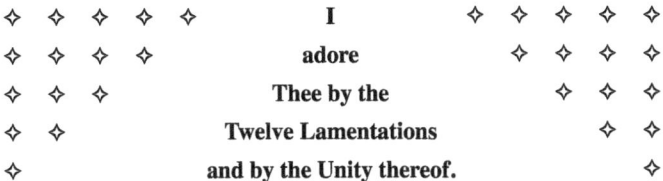

        I
      adore
    Thee by the
  Twelve Lamentations
and by the Unity thereof.

1. O woe unto me, my God, woe unto me; for all my song is as the dirge of the sea that moans about a corpse, lapping most mournfully against the dead shore in the darkness. Yet in the sob of the wind do I hear Thy name, that quickeneth the cold lips of death to life.

2. O woe unto me, my God, woe unto me; for all my praise is as the song of a bird that is ensnared in the network of the winds, and cast adown the drowning depths of night. Yet in the faltering notes of my music do I mark the melody of universal truth.

3. O woe unto me, my God, woe unto me; for all my works are as a coiled-up sleeper who hath overslept the day, even the dawn that hovereth as a hawk in the void. Yet in the gloom of mine awakening do I see, across the breasts of night, Thy shadowed form.

4. O woe unto me, my God, woe unto me; for all my labours are as weary oxen laggard and sore stricken with the goad, ploughing black furrows across the white fields of light. Yet in the scrawling trail of their slow toil do I descry the golden harvest of Thine effulgence.

5. O woe unto me, my God, woe unto me; for all the hope of my heart hath been ravished as the body of a virgin that is fallen into the hands of riotous robbers. Yet in the outrage of mine innocence do I disclose the clear manna of Thy purity.

6. O woe unto me, my God, woe unto me; for all the passion of my love is mazed as the bewildered eyes of a youth, who should wake to find his beloved fled away. Yet in the crumpled couch of lust do I behold an imprint the sigil of Thy name.

7. O woe unto me, my God, woe unto me; for all the joy of my days lies dishonoured as the spangle-veil'd Virgin of night torn and trampled by the sun-lashed stallions of Dawn. Yet in the frenzy of their couplings do I tremble forth the pearly dew of ecstatic light.

8. O woe unto me, my God, woe unto me; for all the aspirations of my heart ruin as in time of earthquake the bare hut of an hermit that he hath built for prayer. Yet from the lightning-struck tower of my reason do I enter Thy house that Thou didst build for me.

9. O woe unto me, my God, woe unto me; for all my joy is as a cloud of dust blown athwart a memory of tears, even across the shadowless brow of the desert. Yet as from the breast of a slave-girl do I pluck the fragrant blossom of Thy Crimson Splendour.

10. O woe unto me, my God, woe unto me; for all the feastings of my flesh have sickened to the wormy hunger of the grave, writhing in the spasms of indolent decay. Yet in the maggots of my corruption do I shadow forth sunlit hosts of crowned eagles.

11. O woe unto me, my God, woe unto me; for all my craft is as an injured arrow, featherless and twisted, that should be loosed from its bow-string by the hands of an infant. Yet in the wayward struggling of its flight do I grip the unwavering courses of Thy wisdom.

12. O woe unto me, my God, woe unto me; for all my faith is as a filthy puddle in the sinister confines of a forest, splashed by the wanton foot of a young gnome. Yet like a wildfire through the trees at nightfall do I divine the distant glimmer of Thine Eye.

13. O woe unto me, my God, woe unto me; for all my life sinks as the western Sun that struggles in the strangling arms of Night, flecked over with the starry foam of her kisses. Yet in the very midnight of my soul do I hold a scarab the signet of Thy name.

> O Glory be unto Thee through all Time
> and through all Space: Glory,
> and Glory upon Glory
> Everlastingly. Amen,
> and Amen, and
> Amen.

The Chapter known as The Twelvefold Bewilderment of God and the Unity thereof

I adore Thee by the Twelve Bewilderments and by the Unity thereof.

1. O what art Thou, O God my God, Thou snow-browed storm that art whirled up in clouds of flame?

O Thou red sword of the thunder!

Thou great blue river of ever-flowing Brightness, over whose breasts creep the star-bannered vessels of night!

O how can I plunge within Thine inscrutable depths, and yet with open eye be lost in the pearly foam of Thine Oblivion?

2. O what art Thou, O God my God, Thou eternal incarnating immortal One?

O Thou welder of life and death!

Thou whose breasts are as the full breasts of a mother, yet in Thy hand Thou carriest the sword of destruction!

O how can I cleave the shield of Thy might as a little wanton child may burst a floating bubble with the breast-feather of a dove?

3. O what art Thou, O God my God, Thou mighty worker laden with the dust of toil?

O Thou little ant of the earth!

Thou great monster who infuriatest the seas, and by their vigour wearest down the strength of the cliffs!

O how can I bind Thee in a spider's web of song, and yet remain one and unconsumed before the raging of Thy nostrils?

4. O what art Thou, O God my God, Thou forked tongue of the purple-throated thunder!

O Thou silver sword of lightning!

Thou who rippest out the fire-bolt from the storm-cloud, as a sorcerer teareth the heart from a black kid!

O how can I possess Thee as the dome of the skies, so that I may fix the keystone of my reason in the arch of Thy forehead?

5. O what art Thou, O God my God, Thou amer-scal'd one whose eyes are set on columns?

O Thou signless seer of all things!

Thou spearless warrior who urgest on Thy steeds and blindest the outer edge of darkness with Thy Glory!

O how can I grasp the whirling wheels of Thy splendour, and yet be not smitten into death by the hurtling fury of Thy chariot?

6. O what art Thou, O God my God, Thou red fire-fang that gnawest the blue limbs of night?

O Thou devouring breath of flame!

Thou illimitable ocean of frenzied air, in whom all is one, a plume cast into a furnace!

O how can I dare to approach and stand before Thee, for I am but as a withered leaf whirled away by the anger of the storm?

7. O what art Thou, O God my God, Thou almighty worker ungirded of slumber?

O Thou Unicorn of the Stars!

Thou tongue of flame burning above the firmament, as a lily that blossometh in the drear desert!

O how can I pluck Thee from the dark bed of Thy birth, and revel like a wine-drenched faun in the banqueting-house of Thy Seigniory?

8. O what art Thou, O God my God, Thou dazzler of the deep obscurity of day?

O Thou golden breast of beauty!

Thou shrivelled udder of the storm-blasted mountains who no longer sucklest the babe-clouds of wind-swept night!

O how can I gaze upon Thy countenance of eld, and yet be not blinded by the black fury of Thy dethroned Majesty?

9. O what art Thou, O God my God, Thou seraph-venom of witch-vengeance enchanted?

O Thou coiled wizardry of stars!

Thou one Lord of life triumphant over death, Thou red rose of love nailed to the cross of golden light!

O how can I die in Thee as sea-foam in the clouds, and yet possess Thee as a frail white mist possesses the stripped limbs of the Sun?

10. O what art Thou, O God my God, Thou soft pearl set in a bow of effulgent light?

O Thou drop of shimmering dew!

Thou surging river of bewildering beauty who speedest as a blue arrow of fire beyond, beyond!

O how can I measure the poisons of Thy limbeck, and yet be for ever transmuted in the athanor of Thine understanding?

11. O what art Thou, O God my God, Thou disrober of the darkness of the Abyss?

O Thou veil'd eye of creation!

Thou soundless voice who, for ever misunderstood, rollest on through the dark abysms of infinity!

O how can I learn to sing the music of Thy name, as a quivering silence above the thundering discord of the tempest?

12. O what art Thou, O God my God, Thou teeming desert of the abundance of night?

O Thou river of unquench'd thirst!

Thou tongueless one who lickest up the dust of death and casteth it forth as the rolling ocean of life!

O how can I possess the still depths of Thy darkness, and yet in Thine embrace all asleep as a child in a bower of lilies?

13. O what art Thou, O God my God, Thou shrouded one veiled in a dazzling effulgence?

O Thou centreless whorl of Time!

Thou illimitable abysm of Righteousness, the lashes of whose eye are as showers of molten suns!

O how can I reflect the light of Thine unity, and melt into Thy Glory as a cloudy chaplet of chalcedony moons?

> O Glory be unto Thee through all Time
> and through all Space: Glory,
> and Glory upon Glory
> Everlastingly. Amen,
> and Amen, and
> Amen.

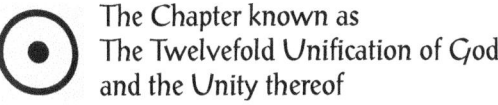

The Chapter known as
The Twelvefold Unification of God
and the Unity thereof

❖ ❖ ❖ ❖ ❖	**I**	❖ ❖ ❖ ❖ ❖
❖ ❖ ❖ ❖	**adore**	❖ ❖ ❖ ❖
❖ ❖ ❖	**Thee by the**	❖ ❖ ❖
❖ ❖	**Twelve Unifications**	❖ ❖
❖	**and by the Unity thereof.**	❖

1. O Thou Unity of all things: as the water that poureth through the fingers of my hand, so art Thou, O God my God. I cannot hold Thee, for Thou art everywhere; lo! though I plunge into the heart of the ocean, there still shall I find Thee, Thou Unity of Unities, Thou Oneness, O Thou perfect Nothingness of Bliss!

2. O Thou Unity of all things: as the hot fire that flameth is too subtle to be held, so art Thou, O God my God. I cannot grasp Thee, for Thou art everywhere; lo! though I hurl me down the scarlet throat of a volcano, there still shall I find Thee, Thou Unity of Unities, Thou Oneness, O Thou perfect Nothingness of Bliss!

3. O Thou Unity of all things: as the moon that waneth and increaseth in the heavens, so art Thou, O God my God. I cannot stay Thee, for Thou art everywhere; lo! though I devour Thee, as a dragon devoureth a kid, there still shall I find Thee, Thou Unity of Unities, Thou Oneness, O Thou perfect Nothingness of Bliss!

4. O Thou Unity of all things: as the dust that danceth over the breast of the desert, so art Thou, O God my God. I cannot hold Thee, for Thou art everywhere; lo! though I lick up with my tongue the bitter salt of the plains, there still shall I find Thee, Thou Unity of Unities, Thou Oneness, O Thou perfect Nothingness of Bliss!

5. O Thou Unity of all things: as the air that bubbleth from the dark depths of the waters, so art Thou, O God my God. I cannot catch Thee, for Thou art everywhere; lo! though I net Thee as a goldfish in a kerchief of silk, there still shall I find Thee, Thou Unity of Unities, Thou Oneness, O Thou perfect Nothingness of Bliss!

6. O Thou Unity of all things: as the cloud that flitteth across the white horns of the moon, so art Thou, O God my God. I cannot pierce Thee, for Thou art everywhere; lo! though I tangle Thee in a witch-gossamer of starlight, there still shall I find Thee, Thou Unity of Unities, Thou Oneness, O Thou perfect Nothingness of Bliss!

7. O Thou Unity of all things: as the star that travelleth along its appointed course, so art Thou, O God my God. I cannot rule Thee, for Thou art everywhere; lo! though I hunt Thee across the blue heavens as a lost comet, there still shall I find Thee, Thou Unity of Unities, Thou Oneness, O Thou perfect Nothingness of Bliss!

8. O Thou Unity of all things: as the lightning that lurketh in the heart of the thunder, so art Thou, O God my God. I cannot search Thee, for Thou art everywhere; lo! though I wed the flaming circle to the enshrouded square, there still shall I find Thee, Thou Unity of Unities, Thou Oneness, O Thou perfect Nothingness of Bliss!

9. O Thou Unity of all things: as the earth that holdeth all precious jewels in her heart, so art Thou, O God my God. I cannot spoil Thee, for Thou art everywhere; lo! though I burrow as a mole in the mountain of Chaos, there still shall I find Thee, Thou Unity of Unities, Thou Oneness, O Thou perfect Nothingness of Bliss!

10. O Thou Unity of all things: as the pole-star that burneth in the centre of the night, so art Thou, O God my God. I cannot hide Thee, for Thou art everywhere; lo! though I turn from Thee at each touch of the lodestone of lust, there still shall I find Thee, Thou Unity of Unities, Thou Oneness, O Thou perfect Nothingness of Bliss!

11. O Thou Unity of all things: as the blue smoke that whirleth up from the altar of life, so art Thou, O God my God. I cannot hold Thee, for Thou art everywhere; lo! though I inter Thee in the sarcophagi of the damned, there still shall I find Thee, Thou Unity of Unities, Thou Oneness, O Thou perfect Nothingness of Bliss!

12. O Thou Unity of all things: as a dark-eyed maiden decked in crimson and precious pearls, so art Thou, O God my God. I cannot hold Thee, for Thou art everywhere; lo! though I strip Thee of Thy gold and scarlet raiment of Self, there still shall I find Thee, Thou Unity of Unities, Thou Oneness, O Thou perfect Nothingness of Bliss!

13. O Thou Unity of all things: as the sun that rolleth through the twelve mansions of the skies, so art Thou, O God my God. I cannot slay Thee, for Thou art everywhere; lo! though I lick up the Boundless Light, The Boundless, and the Not, there still shall I find Thee, Thou Unity of Unities, Thou Oneness, O Thou perfect Nothingness of Bliss!

>O Glory be unto Thee through all Time
>and through all Space: Glory,
>and Glory upon Glory
>Everlastingly. Amen,
>and Amen, and
>Amen.

The Chapter known as
The Hundred and Sixty-Nine Cries of God
and the Unity thereof

```
  ✧  ✧  ✧  ✧  ✧  ✧        I         ✧  ✧  ✧  ✧  ✧  ✧
  ✧  ✧  ✧  ✧  ✧        adore           ✧  ✧  ✧  ✧  ✧
  ✧  ✧  ✧  ✧         Thee by the         ✧  ✧  ✧  ✧
  ✧  ✧  ✧        Hundred and Sixty-         ✧  ✧  ✧
  ✧  ✧         Nine Cries of Adoration         ✧  ✧
  ✧          and by the Unity thereof.            ✧
```

O Thou Dragon-prince of the air, that art drunk on the blood of the sunsets! I adore Thee, Evoe! I adore Thee, IAO!

O Thou Unicorn of the storm, that art crested above the purple air! I adore Thee, Evoe! I adore Thee, IAO!

O Thou burning sword of passion, that art tempered on the anvil of flesh! I adore Thee, Evoe! I adore Thee, IAO!

O Thou slimy lust of the grave, that art tangled in the roots of the tree! I adore Thee, Evoe! I adore Thee, IAO!

O Thou smoke-shrouded sword of flame, that art ensheathed in the bowels of earth! I adore Thee, Evoe! I adore Thee, IAO!

O Thou scented grove of wild vines, that art trampled by the white feet of love! I adore Thee, Evoe! I adore Thee, IAO!

O Thou golden sheaf of desires, that art bound by a fair wisp of poppies! I adore Thee, Evoe! I adore Thee, IAO!

O Thou molten comet of gold, that art seen through the wizard's glass of Space! I adore Thee, Evoe! I adore Thee, IAO!

O Thou shrill song of the eunuch, that art heard behind the curtain of shame! I adore Thee, Evoe! I adore Thee, IAO!

O Thou bright star of the morning, that art seen betwixt the breasts of night! I adore Thee, Evoe! I adore Thee, IAO!

O Thou lidless eye of the world, that art seen from the sapphire veil of space! I adore Thee, Evoe! I adore Thee, IAO!

O Thou smiling mouth of the dawn, that art freed from the laughter of the night! I adore Thee, Evoe! I adore Thee, IAO!

O Thou dazzling star-point of hope, that burnest over oceans of despair! I adore Thee, Evoe! I adore Thee, IAO!

O Thou naked virgin of love, that art caught in a net of wild roses! I adore Thee, Evoe! I adore Thee, IAO!

O Thou iron turret of death, that art rusted with the bright blood of war! I adore Thee, Evoe! I adore Thee, IAO!

O Thou bubbling wine-cup of joy, that foamest like the cauldron of murder! I adore Thee, Evoe! I adore Thee, IAO!

O Thou icy trail of the moon, that art traced in the veins of the onyx! I adore Thee, Evoe! I adore Thee, IAO!

O Thou frenzied hunter of love, that art slain by the twisted horns of lust! I adore Thee, Evoe! I adore Thee, IAO!

O Thou frozen book of the seas, that art graven by the swords of the sun! I adore Thee, Evoe! I adore Thee, IAO!

O Thou flashing opal of light, that art wrapped in the robes of the rainbow! I adore Thee, Evoe! I adore Thee, IAO!

O Thou purple mist of the hills, that hideth shepherds from the wanton moon! I adore Thee, Evoe! I adore Thee, IAO!

O Thou low moan of fainting maids, that art caught up in the strong sobs of love! I adore Thee, Evoe! I adore Thee, IAO!

O Thou fleeting beam of delight, that lurkest within the spear-thrusts of dawn! I adore Thee, Evoe! I adore Thee, IAO!

O Thou golden wine of the sun, that art poured over the dark breasts of night! I adore Thee, Evoe! I adore Thee, IAO!

O Thou fragrance of sweet flowers, that art wafted over blue fields of air! I adore Thee, Evoe! I adore Thee, IAO!

O Thou mighty bastion of faith, that withstandest all the breachers of doubt! I adore Thee, Evoe! I adore Thee, IAO!

O Thou silver horn of the moon, that gorest the red flank of the morning! I adore Thee, Evoe! I adore Thee, IAO!

O Thou grey glory of twilight, that art the hermaphrodite triumphant! I adore Thee, Evoe! I adore Thee, IAO!

O Thou thirsty mouth of the wind, that art maddened by the foam of the sea! I adore Thee, Evoe! I adore Thee, IAO!

O Thou couch of rose-leaf desires, that art crumpled by the vine and the fir! I adore Thee, Evoe! I adore Thee, IAO!

O Thou bird-sweet river of Love, that warblest through the pebbly gorge of Life! I adore Thee, Evoe! I adore Thee, IAO!

O Thou golden network of stars, that art girt about the cold breasts of Night! I adore Thee, Evoe! I adore Thee, IAO!

O Thou mad whirlwind of laughter, that art meshed in the wild locks of folly! I adore Thee, Evoe! I adore Thee, IAO!

O Thou white hand of Creation, that holdest up the dying head of Death! I adore Thee, Evoe! I adore Thee, IAO!

O Thou purple tongue of Twilight, that dost lap up the lucent milk of Day! I adore Thee, Evoe! I adore Thee, IAO!

O Thou thunderbolts of Science, that flashest from the dark clouds of Magic! I adore Thee, Evoe! I adore Thee, IAO!

O Thou red rose of the Morning, that glowest in the bosom of the Night! I adore Thee, Evoe! I adore Thee, IAO!

O Thou flaming globe of Glory, that art caught up in the arms of the sun! I adore Thee, Evoe! I adore Thee, IAO!

O Thou silver arrow of hope, that art shot from the arc of the rainbow! I adore Thee, Evoe! I adore Thee, IAO!

O Thou starry virgin of Night, that art strained to the arms of the morning! I adore Thee, Evoe! I adore Thee, IAO!

O Thou sworded soldier of life, that art sucked down in the quicksands of death! I adore Thee, Evoe! I adore Thee, IAO!

O Thou bronze blast of the trumpet, that rollest over emerald-tipped spears! I adore Thee, Evoe! I adore Thee, IAO!

O Thou opal mist of the sea, that art sucked up by the beams of the sun! I adore Thee, Evoe! I adore Thee, IAO!

O Thou red worm of formation, that art lifted by the white whorl of love! I adore Thee, Evoe! I adore Thee, IAO!

O Thou mighty anvil of Time, that outshowerest the bright sparks of life! I adore Thee, Evoe! I adore Thee, IAO!

O Thou red cobra of desire, that art unhooded by the hands of girls! I adore Thee, Evoe! I adore Thee, IAO!

O Thou curling billow of joy, whose fingers caress the limbs of the world! I adore Thee, Evoe! I adore Thee, IAO!

O Thou emerald vulture of Truth, that art perched upon the vast tree of life! I adore Thee, Evoe! I adore Thee, IAO!

O Thou lonely eagle of night, that drinkest at the moist lips of the moon! I adore Thee, Evoe! I adore Thee, IAO!

O Thou wild daughter of Chaos, that art ravished by the strong son of law! I adore Thee, Evoe! I adore Thee, IAO!

O Thou ghostly night of terror, that art slaughtered in the blood of the dawn! I adore Thee, Evoe! I adore Thee, IAO!

O Thou poppied nectar of sleep, that art curled in the still womb of slumber! I adore Thee, Evoe! I adore Thee, IAO!

O Thou burning rapture of girls, that disport in the sunset of passion! I adore Thee, Evoe! I adore Thee, IAO!

O Thou molten ocean of stars, that art a crown for the forehead of day! I adore Thee, Evoe! I adore Thee, IAO!

O Thou little brook in the hills, like an asp betwixt the breasts of a girl! I adore Thee, Evoe! I adore Thee, IAO!

O Thou mighty oak of magic, that art rooted in the mountain of life! I adore Thee, Evoe! I adore Thee, IAO!

O Thou sparkling network of pearls, that art woven of the waves by the moon! I adore Thee, Evoe! I adore Thee, IAO!

O Thou wanton sword-blade of life, that art sheathed by the harlot call'd Death! I adore Thee, Evoe! I adore Thee, IAO!

O Thou mist-clad spirit of spring, that art unrob'd by the hands of the wind! I adore Thee, Evoe! I adore Thee, IAO!

O Thou sweet perfume of desire, that art wafted through the valleys of love! I adore Thee, Evoe! I adore Thee, IAO!

O Thou sparkling wine-cup of light, whose foaming is the heart's blood of the stars! I adore Thee, Evoe! I adore Thee, IAO!

O Thou silver sword of madness, that art smitten through the midden of life! I adore Thee, Evoe! I adore Thee, IAO!

O Thou hooded vulture of night, that art glutted on the entrails of day! I adore Thee, Evoe! I adore Thee, IAO!

O Thou pearl-grey arch of the world, whose keystone is the ecstasy of man! I adore Thee, Evoe! I adore Thee, IAO!

O Thou silken web of movement, that art blown through the atoms of matter! I adore Thee, Evoe! I adore Thee, IAO!

O Thou rush-strewn threshold of joy, that art lost in the quicksands of reason! I adore Thee, Evoe! I adore Thee, IAO!

O Thou wild vision of Beauty, but half seen betwixt the cusps of the moon! I adore Thee, Evoe! I adore Thee, IAO!

O Thou pearl cloud of the sunset, that art caught up in a murderer's hand! I adore Thee, Evoe! I adore Thee, IAO!

O Thou rich vintage of slumber that art crushed from the bud of the poppy! I adore Thee, Evoe! I adore Thee, IAO!

O Thou great boulder of rapture, that leapest adown the mountains of joy! I adore Thee, Evoe! I adore Thee, IAO!

O Thou breather-out of the winds, that art snared in the drag-net of reason! I adore Thee, Evoe! I adore Thee, IAO!

O Thou purple breast of the storm, that art scarred by the teeth of the lightning! I adore Thee, Evoe! I adore Thee, IAO!

O Thou Pillar of phosphor foam, that Leviathan spouteth from's nostrils! I adore Thee, Evoe! I adore Thee, IAO!

O Thou song of the harp of life, that chantest forth the perfection of death! I adore Thee, Evoe! I adore Thee, IAO!

O Thou veilèd beam of the stars, that art tangled in the tresses of night! I adore Thee, Evoe! I adore Thee, IAO!

O Thou flashing shield of the sun, as a discus hurled by the hand of Space! I adore Thee, Evoe! I adore Thee, IAO!

O Thou ribald shout of laughter, that echoest among the tombs of death! I adore Thee, Evoe! I adore Thee, IAO!

O Thou unfailing cruse of joy, that art filled with the tears of the fallen! I adore Thee, Evoe! I adore Thee, IAO!

O Thou burning lust of the moon, that art clothed in the mist of the ocean! I adore Thee, Evoe! I adore Thee, IAO!

O Thou one measure of all things, that art Dam of the great order of worlds! I adore Thee, Evoe! I adore Thee, IAO!

O Thou frail virgin of Eden, that art ravished to the abode of Hell! I adore Thee, Evoe! I adore Thee, IAO!

O Thou dark forest of wonder, the art tangled in a gold web of dew! I adore Thee, Evoe! I adore Thee, IAO!

O Thou tortured shriek of the storm, that art whirled up through the leaves of the woods! I adore Thee, Evoe! I adore Thee, IAO!

O Thou dazzling opal of light, that flamest in the crumbling skull of space! I adore Thee, Evoe! I adore Thee, IAO!

O Thou red knife of destruction, that art sheathed in the bowels of order! I adore Thee, Evoe! I adore Thee, IAO!

O Thou storm-drunk breath of the winds, that pant in the bosom of the mountains! I adore Thee, Evoe! I adore Thee, IAO!

O Thou loud bell of rejoicing, that art smitten by the hammer of woe! I adore Thee, Evoe! I adore Thee, IAO!

O Thou red rose of the sunset, that witherest on the altar of night! I adore Thee, Evoe! I adore Thee, IAO!

O Thou bright vision of sunbeams, that burnest in a flagon of topaz! I adore Thee, Evoe! I adore Thee, IAO!

O Thou virgin lily of night, that spoutest between the lips of a corpse! I adore Thee, Evoe! I adore Thee, IAO!

O Thou blue helm of destruction, that art winged with the lightnings of madness! I adore Thee, Evoe! I adore Thee, IAO!

O Thou voice of the heaving seas, that tremblest in the grey of the twilight! I adore Thee, Evoe! I adore Thee, IAO!

O Thou unfolder of heaven, red-winged as an eagle at sunrise! I adore Thee, Evoe! I adore Thee, IAO!

O Thou curling tongue of red flame, athirst on the nipple of my passion! I adore Thee, Evoe! I adore Thee, IAO!

O Thou outrider of the sun, that spurrest the bloody flanks of the wind! I adore Thee, Evoe! I adore Thee, IAO!

O Thou dancer with gilded nails, that unbraidest the star-hair of the night! I adore Thee, Evoe! I adore Thee, IAO!

O Thou moonlit pearl of rapture, clasped fast in the silver hand of the Dawn! I adore Thee, Evoe! I adore Thee, IAO!

O Thou wanton mother of love, that art mistress of the children of men! I adore Thee, Evoe! I adore Thee, IAO!

O Thou crimson fountain of blood, that spoutest from the heart of Creation! I adore Thee, Evoe! I adore Thee, IAO!

O Thou warrior eye of the sun, that shooteth death from the berylline Byss! I adore Thee, Evoe! I adore Thee, IAO!

O Thou Witch's hell-broth of hate, that boilest in the white cauldron of love! I adore Thee, Evoe! I adore Thee, IAO!

O Thou Ribbon of Northern Lights, that bindest the elfin tresses of night! I adore Thee, Evoe! I adore Thee, IAO!

O Thou red sword of the Twilight, that art rusted with the blood of noon! I adore Thee, Evoe! I adore Thee, IAO!

O Thou sacrificer of Dawn, that wearest the chasuble of sunset! I adore Thee, Evoe! I adore Thee, IAO!

O Thou bloodshot eye of lightning, glowering beneath the eyebrows of thunder! I adore Thee, Evoe! I adore Thee, IAO!

O Thou four-square Crown of Nothing, that circlest the destruction of worlds! I adore Thee, Evoe! I adore Thee, IAO!

O Thou bloodhound whirlwind of lust, that art unleashed by the first kiss of love! I adore Thee, Evoe! I adore Thee, IAO!

O Thou wondrous chalice of light, uplifted by the Mænads of Dawn! I adore Thee, Evoe! I adore Thee, IAO!

O Thou fecund opal of death, that sparklest through a sea of mother-of-pearl! I adore Thee, Evoe! I adore Thee, IAO!

O Thou crimson rose of the Dawn, that art fastened in the dark locks of Night! I adore Thee, Evoe! I adore Thee, IAO!

O Thou pink nipple of Being, thrust deep into the black mouth of Chaos! I adore Thee, Evoe! I adore Thee, IAO!

O Thou vampire Queen of the Flesh, wound as a snake around the throats of men! I adore Thee, Evoe! I adore Thee, IAO!

O Thou tender nest of dove's down, built up betwixt the hawk's claws of the Night! I adore Thee, Evoe! I adore Thee, IAO!

O Thou concubine of Matter, anointed with love-nard of Motion! I adore Thee, Evoe! I adore Thee, IAO!

O Thou flame-tipp'd bolt of Morning, that art shot out from the cross-bow of Night! I adore Thee, Evoe! I adore Thee, IAO!

O Thou frail blue-bell of Moonlight, that art lost in the gardens of the Stars! I adore Thee, Evoe! I adore Thee, IAO!

O Thou tall mast of wreck'd Chaos, that art crowned by the white lamp of Cosmos! I adore Thee, Evoe! I adore Thee, IAO!

O Thou pearly eyelid of Day, that art closed by the finger of Evening! I adore Thee, Evoe! I adore Thee, IAO!

O Thou wild anarch of the Hills, pale glooming above the mists of the Earth! I adore Thee, Evoe! I adore Thee, IAO!

O Thou moonlit peak of pleasure, that art crowned by viper tongues of forked flame! I adore Thee, Evoe! I adore Thee, IAO!

O Thou wolfish head of the winds, that frighteth the snow-white lamb of winter! I adore Thee, Evoe! I adore Thee, IAO!

O Thou dew-lit nymph of the Dawn, that swoonest in the satyr arms of the Sun! I adore Thee, Evoe! I adore Thee, IAO!

O Thou mad abode of kisses, that art lit by the fat of murdered fiends! I adore Thee, Evoe! I adore Thee, IAO!

O Thou sleeping lust of the Storm, that art flame-gorg'd as a flint full of fire! I adore Thee, Evoe! I adore Thee, IAO!

O Thou soft dew of the Evening, that art drunk up by the mist of the Night! I adore Thee, Evoe! I adore Thee, IAO!

O Thou wounded son of the West, that gushest out Thy blood on the heavens! I adore Thee, Evoe! I adore Thee, IAO!

O Thou burning tower of fire, that art set up in the midst of the seas! I adore Thee, Evoe! I adore Thee, IAO!

O Thou unvintageable dew, that art moist upon the lips of the Morn! I adore Thee, Evoe! I adore Thee, IAO!

O Thou silver crescent of love, that burnest over the dark helm of War! I adore Thee, Evoe! I adore Thee, IAO!

O Thou snow-white ram of the Dawn, the art slain by the lion of the noon! I adore Thee, Evoe! I adore Thee, IAO!

O Thou crimson spear-point of life, that art thrust through the dark bowels of Time! I adore Thee, Evoe! I adore Thee, IAO!

O Thou black waterspout of Death, that whirlest, whelmest the tall ship of Life! I adore Thee, Evoe! I adore Thee, IAO!

O Thou mighty chain of events, that art strained betwixt Cosmos and Chaos! I adore Thee, Evoe! I adore Thee, IAO!

O Thou towering eagre of lust, that art heaped up by the moon-breasts of youth! I adore Thee, Evoe! I adore Thee, IAO!

O Thou serpent-crown of green light, that art wound round the dark forehead of Death! I adore Thee, Evoe! I adore Thee, IAO!

O Thou crimson vintage of Life, that art poured into the jar of the Grave! I adore Thee, Evoe! I adore Thee, IAO!

O Thou waveless Ocean of Peace, that sleepest beneath the wild heart of man! I adore Thee, Evoe! I adore Thee, IAO!

O Thou whirling skirt of the stars, that art swathed round the limbs of the Æthyr! I adore Thee, Evoe! I adore Thee, IAO!

O Thou snow-white chalice of Love, thou art filled up with the red lusts of Man! I adore Thee, Evoe! I adore Thee, IAO!

O Thou fragrant garden of Joy, firm-set betwixt the breasts of the morning! I adore Thee, Evoe! I adore Thee, IAO!

O Thou pearly fountain of Life, that spoutest up in the black court of Death! I adore Thee, Evoe! I adore Thee, IAO!

O Thou brindle hound of the Night, with thy nose to the sleuth of the Sunset! I adore Thee, Evoe! I adore Thee, IAO!

O Thou leprous claw of the ghoul, that coaxes the babe from its chaste cradle! I adore Thee, Evoe! I adore Thee, IAO!

O Thou assassin word of law, that art written in ruin of earthquakes! I adore Thee, Evoe! I adore Thee, IAO!

O Thou trembling breast of the night, that gleamest with a rosary of moons! I adore Thee, Evoe! I adore Thee, IAO!

O Thou Holy Sphinx of rebirth, that crouchest in the black desert of death! I adore Thee, Evoe! I adore Thee, IAO!

O Thou diadem of the suns, that art the knot of this red web of worlds! I adore Thee, Evoe! I adore Thee, IAO!

O Thou ravished river of law, that outpourest the arcanum of Life! I adore Thee, Evoe! I adore Thee, IAO!

O Thou glimmering tongue of day, that art sucked into the blue lips of Night! I adore Thee, Evoe! I adore Thee, IAO!

O Thou Queen-Bee of Heaven's hive, that smearest thy thighs with honey of Hell! I adore Thee, Evoe! I adore Thee, IAO!

O Thou scarlet dragon of flame, enmeshed in the web of a spider! I adore Thee, Evoe! I adore Thee, IAO!

O Thou magic symbol of light, that art frozen on the black book of blood! I adore Thee, Evoe! I adore Thee, IAO!

O Thou swathed image of Death, that art hidden in the coffin of joy! I adore Thee, Evoe! I adore Thee, IAO!

O Thou red breast of the sunset, that pantest for the ravishment of Night! I adore Thee, Evoe! I adore Thee, IAO!

O Thou serpent of malachite, that baskest in a desert of turquoise! I adore Thee, Evoe! I adore Thee, IAO!

O Thou fierce whirlpool of passion, that art sucked up by the mouth of the sun! I adore Thee, Evoe! I adore Thee, IAO!

O Thou green cockatrice of Hell, that art coiled around the finger of Fate! I adore Thee, Evoe! I adore Thee, IAO!

O Thou lambent laughter of fire, that art wounded round the heart of the waters! I adore Thee, Evoe! I adore Thee, IAO!

O Thou gorilla blizzard Air, that tearest out Earth's tresses by the roots! I adore Thee, Evoe! I adore Thee, IAO!

O Thou reveller of Spirit, that carousest in the halls of Matter! I adore Thee, Evoe! I adore Thee, IAO!

O Thou red-lipped Vampire of Life, that drainest blood from the black Mount of Death! I adore Thee, Evoe! I adore Thee, IAO!

O Thou little lark of Beyond, that art heard in the dark groves of knowledge! I adore Thee, Evoe! I adore Thee, IAO!

O Thou summer softness of lips, that glow hot with the scarlet of passion! I adore Thee, Evoe! I adore Thee, IAO!

O Thou pearly foam of the grape, that art flecked with the roses of love! I adore Thee, Evoe! I adore Thee, IAO!

O Thou frenzied hand of the seas, that unfurlest the black Banner of Storm! I adore Thee, Evoe! I adore Thee, IAO!

O Thou shrouded book of the dead, that art sealed with the seven souls of man! I adore Thee, Evoe! I adore Thee, IAO!

O Thou writhing frenzy of love, that art knotted like the grid-flames of Hell! I adore Thee, Evoe! I adore Thee, IAO!

O Thou primal birth-ring of thought, that dost encircle the thumb of the soul! I adore Thee, Evoe! I adore Thee, IAO!

O Thou blind flame of Nothingness, as a crown upon my brow! I adore Thee, Evoe! I adore Thee, IAO!

> O Glory be unto Thee through all Time
> and through all Space: Glory,
> and Glory upon Glory
> Everlastingly. Amen,
> and Amen, and
> Amen.

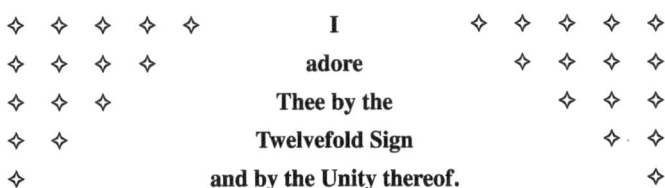

The Chapter known as
The Unconsciousness of God
and the Unity thereof

✧	✧	✧	✧	✧	I	✧	✧	✧	✧	✧
✧	✧	✧	✧		adore		✧	✧	✧	✧
✧	✧	✧			Thee by the			✧	✧	✧
✧	✧				**Twelvefold Sign**				✧	✧
✧					**and by the Unity thereof.**					✧

12. The Light of my Life is as the light of two moons, one rising and the other setting, one increasing and the other waning; the one growing fat as the groweth lean, like a paunchy thief sucking dry a skin of amber wine. Yet though the light of the first devoureth the light of the second, nevertheless the light of the second disgorgeth the light of the first, so that there is neither the desire of light nor the need of light–all being as a woven twilight of day and night, a madness of mingling moons. Yet I behold!

11. Now mine eyes are seven, and are as stars about a star; and the lids of mine eyes are fourteen, two to each eye. Also have I seven arms to do the bidding of the seven eyes; and each arm hath an hand of three fingers, so that I may rule the great ocean and burn it up with the Spirit of Flame, and that I may drown the fire in the Abode of the Waters. Thus I am rendered naked; for neither flame nor water can clothe me; therefore am I as a breath of wind blown over an Earth of Adamant, that knoweth neither sorrow nor rejoicing; then do I abide as a River of Light between Night of Chaos and the Day of Creation.

10. Two are the moons of my madness, like the horns on the head of a goat. And between them burneth a pyramid of flame, which consumeth neither but blindeth both, so that the one beholdeth not the other.

Notwithstanding, when the one is lost in the water, and the other is burnt up in the flame, they become united in the form of a woman fashioned of Earth and of Air, who without husband is yet mother of many sons.

9. Now the Sons are in truth but one Son; and the one Son but a daughter draped and never naked; for her mother is naked, therefore is she robed. And she is called the Light of my Love, for she is concealed and cannot be seen, as the Sun burneth over her and drowneth her in fire, whilst below her surgeth the sea, whose waves are as flames of water. When thou hast licked up the ocean thou shalt not see her because of the fire; and when thou hast swallowed the Sun surely shall the waters be driven from thee, so that though the fire be thine the water hath sipped thee, as a dog its leash. Yet the path is straight.

8. Along it shalt thou journey, and then shalt thou learn that the fear of death is the blood of the world. So the woman dressed herself in the shrouds of the dead, and decked herself with the bones of the fallen; and all feared her, therefore they lived. But she feared life; therefore she wove a dew-moon in her tangled hair as a sign of the fickleness of Death, and wept tears of bitter sorrow that she should live in the blossom of her youth. And her tears crept like scorpions down her cheeks, and sped away in the darkness like serpents; and for each serpent came there an eagle which did carry it away.

7. "Why weep?" said the Balance swinging to the left. "Why laugh?" said the Balance swinging to the right. "Why not remain still?" answered the Hand that held the Balance. And the Balance replied: "Because on my right hand laughs Death and on my left weeps a Virgin."

6. Then the voice of the Hand said to the girl: "Why weep? And the maid answered: "Because Death maketh jest of my life." Then the Hand stayed the Balance, and at once the girl saw that she was Death, and that

Death that had sat opposite her was in truth a motherless babe. So she took the child she had conceived in the arms of fear, and went her way laughing.

5. And the infant grew strong; yet its strength was in its weakness; and though to look at it from before was to look upon a man-child, from behind it was a little girl with golden hair. Now, when the child wished to tempt a maid he faced and approached her; and when the child wished to tempt a man she turned her back on him and fled.

4. But one day the child met, at the self-same hour, Love; and the man, seeing a woman, approached her eagerly, and the woman, seeing a man, fled, so that he might capture her. Thus it came about that a child met the child and wondered, not knowing that the child had lost the child. So it was that they walked side by side.

3. Then that part of the child that was man loved and lusted for that part of the child that was woman; and each knew not that each was the other, and felt that they were two and yet one, nevertheless one and yet two. And when one said: "Who art thou?" the other answered at the self-same moment: "Who am I?"

2. Soon becoming perplexed if I were Thou, or if Thou were I, it came about that the I mingled with the Thou, and the Thou with the I, so that six added to ten became sixteen, which is felicity: for it is the interplay of the elements. Four are the elements that make man, and four are the elements that make woman. Thus was a child reborn.

1. But though the man ruleth the woman, and the woman ruleth the man, the Child ruleth both its mother and father, and being five is Emperor over the kingdom of their hearts. To its father it giveth four, and to its mother it giveth four, yet it remaineth five, for it hath of its father and half

and of its mother an half; but in itself it is equal to both its father and its mother; for it is father of fathers and mother of mothers.

0. Therefore it is One Whole, and not two halves; and being One is Thirteen, which is called Nothing when it is All-things.

Amen
without lie,
and Amen of Amen,
and Amen of Amen of Amen.

The Greek Cross of the Zodiac

- ♈ Emerald on Scarlet
- ♉ Greenish Blue on Orange-Red
- ♊ Royal Blue on Orange
- ♋ Indigo on Amber
- ♌ Violet on Greenish-Yellow
- ♍ Crimson on Yellow-Green
- ♎ Scarlet on Emerald
- ♏ Orange-Red on Greenish Blue
- ♐ Orange on Royal Blue
- ♑ Amber on Indigo
- ♒ Greenish-Yellow on Violet
- ♓ Yellow-Green on Crimson

Spirit. Black on White
Serpent. Azure, with Golden Scales
Border. Gold

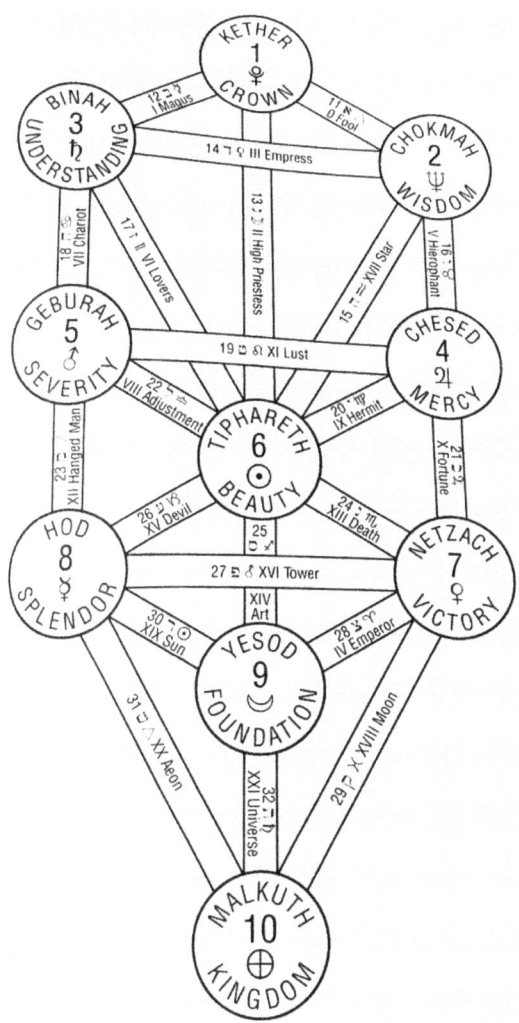

THE TREE OF LIFE

Afterword:
Pathworking Practice

Nancy Wasserman

✺

*O thou that settest out upon The Path, false is the
Phantom that thou seekest. When thou hast it
thou shalt know all bitterness, thy teeth fixed in
the Sodom-Apple.*

*Thus hast thou been lured along That Path, whose
terror else had driven thee far away.*

*O thou that stridest upon the middle of The Path, no
phantoms mock thee. For the stride's sake thou stridest.*

*Thus are thou lured upon That Path, whose
fascination else had driven thee far away.*

*O thou that drawest toward the End of The Path,
effort is no more. Faster and faster dost thou fall;
thy weariness is changed in Ineffable Rest.
For there is no Thou upon That Path; thou
hast become the Way.*

(from *The Book of Lies*, Aleister Crowley)

Pathworking is a means of exploring the universe in a systematic manner. As with any expedition, the most value is found by keeping an open mind and a sense of humor. Using the Kabbalistic Tree of Life as a map, the student can embark on a profound journey of self-discovery. In my opinion, the greatest benefit of these practices is an opening of the mind and an increased ability to focus the psyche. Pathworking differs from simple astral projection in that it allows the student a definite structure to work within. An individual's symbol sets are subjective, but there are certain key elements that should be common to all student's experiences.

The Tree of Life utilizes two main symbol sets, Tarot and Astrology. The Tarot is used to describe the energy channels or paths leading between the spheres of the Sephiroth. Both the Sepiroth and paths have astrological attributions; these are the focus of Liber 963, *The Treasure House of Images*.

Preliminary Practices

To make your Pathworking experiences truly meaningful, it is extremely important to build your astral body into as strong and resilient a magical weapons you can make it. Every modern teacher from Madame Blavatsky to William Gray, and every esoteric school from the Golden Dawn to Wicca and Scientology, include rigorous training in, and emphasis on, controlling and working with this subtle part of ourselves. Aleister Crowley said in *Magick in Theory and Practice* "The magician can hardly take too much trouble to develop this power in himself."

While it is true that Pathworking practices help train your Body of Light and sharpen your abilities on the astral plane, it is also true that before you can trust your vision and experiences, your magical body must become defined, with the dexterity required to navigate the Empyrean realms. The astral plane is one of illusion and deception–but a skilled magician is able to discern between the truth and the illusions of that most tenuous, ever-shifting place. With patience and persistence, anyone can gain the skills to experience it. After the basic skills have been mastered, the student can fully experience the multidimensional riches that Pathworking has to offer.

Here are some suggestions for basic practices to build one's Body of Light prior to actual Pathworking. I have found that every person discovers certain unique, personal methods and means to formulate the Body of Light and project into the higher planes, but the following are a good starting point.

1. The Diary–Establish a regular practice of keeping diary entries so you may learn from past experiences. It is especially important to become proficient in dream recall. Like dreams, details of Pathworking on the Magical and Astral planes tend to leave the conscious mind very rapidly. Unless you make a habit of recording your dreams as soon as you are awake, the most you are left with is an overview of the experience without details. Use the diary system with Pathworking and astral projection exercises in the same way–write down your experiences in detail immediately after you are awake. These details (although they may seem unimportant at the time), are essential for verifying and validating your experiences (whether you are working with a group, one-on-one with an instructor, or as a solitary practitioner.). In fact, verifying your experiences is a crucial part of your magical training. It will separate the products of your imagination from your "real" experiences and allow you to carefully analyze the practice. Remember that in the Western system, we prefer to use a more evidence-based approach–you should be able to back up your experiences with the correct corresponding symbol set. Which brings us to point number 2.

2. The Kabbalah–Symbols on the astral plane are varied, rich and can be very subjective–up to a point. Certain elements will bear a common thread, so it is very important to STUDY, STUDY, STUDY your Kabbalah! Although it is a complicated system, the practice gets much easier with time. It does wonders for improving the memory and it is exquisitely logical. More importantly, it is the roadmap to the Magical Universe. When you become comfortable with the basic correspondences, Kabbalah is foolproof.

3. Banishing/Purification Rituals–It is essential to perform a complete magical banishing ritual *before* and *after* any astral work, especially Pathworking. If you are unfamiliar with formal banishing rituals proceed no further in this work until you become proficient in at least one type of banishing ritual. The Lesser Banishing Ritual of the Pentagram (LBR) which you can find on page 125 of this book is the most useful. For the practitioner of Western Magick, it is simple, straightforward, powerful and suits a variety of purposes. As luck would have it, it is also easily performed by beginners, which makes it just about perfect.

Although the phrase "Pathworking" is a relatively modern expression, this concept has existed for many years under different names. For example, at the turn of the 20th century it was called "Scrying in the Spirit Vision." Regardless of the nomenclature, learning to formulate the Body of Light, and the practice of rising on the magical planes, are important parts of spiritual development. The serious student should devote serious effort to arm herself with a strong Astral Body and practice using it enough to feel confident while executing the practices. Such intensive work requires the clean vibration and protected environment a formal banishing offers. "Smudging" with sage or other herbal incense, floor washes, bell-ringing, and other less ritualized actions are insufficient for this type of work–although one may include them as part of the banishing/purifying process.

Astral Projection

Banishing performed, diary by your side, settle yourself in a comfortable but upright position. As tempting as lying prone may be, it is far too easy to relax too deeply or fall asleep. This will make it harder to come back into "waking" consciousness and much harder for you to record your experiences. It is easier to come out of your astral state if you are sitting up. Remember that the key is to relax the body while keeping the mind awake. When you begin these exercises, unless you are used to meditating for periods of time, your body may become uncomfortable. With consistent practice, your body will get used to sitting and this will no longer be a problem.

After you are in a comfortable but firm position, relax your physical body and focus on your breathing. As your body calms and your muscles and joints stretch open, your mind will relax, and become more sensitive. As you continue breathing, become aware of your subtle body. With your out-breaths, begin to "consciously" and *gently* transfer your thoughts to your subtle body. Let your brain function from there. Feel as some of your emotions center themselves there. Think about and be aware of them. Finally, breath out and project fully into your subtle body.

Your consciousness being transferred to your subtle body, see, hear, smell, taste and feel from there. Note the changes in perception between your physical and astral body. Do your surroundings look the same? What do you notice with your astral ears that you never heard on the physical? Does that rose smell the same? How does the rug feel? Do you have a sense of gravity? Temperature? Try to sense and understand the energy that holds the Fine Body together. What does your Astral Body look like?

Regardless of the type of astral work you are doing, be very aware of your thoughts, emotions and sensations. Try to keep a careful record of them. I have found that most of them will change over time (just like in "real" life). Once you are consciously aware of its limits and powers, allow your Astral Body to walk around your Circle. Try to perform various tasks while on that level. Formulate talismans, sigils, weapons, and other symbols you think you will need during the course of your working. One of the most important things you can do during this stage of development is to construct as astral temple. Be meticulous and detailed. Sketch it out in your diary. For detailed instructions and exact methods described by Aleister Crowley, please refer to *Liber O*, which we have included on page 113 of this text.

When I was beginning these practices, my main difficulty was transferring my "conscious" thoughts out of my physical body and keeping them in the astral. It was very easy to observe my astral body and perform tasks on the astral as an observer. It was relatively easy to transfer my "conscious" thoughts and think on the astral plane, but it was really difficult to remember to *keep* my conscious there. I would often find myself *observing* rather than *experiencing* the astral. I think this is a relatively common problem and it represents a complete break in the process. Months of frustrating practice resolved this problem. Don't give up. Remember that work on the astral plane is active rather than passive.

Once you are completely comfortable in your astral body, allow your subtle body to rise in the air and to the astral plane. You will find this step to be relatively easy if you have perfected the practice of keeping your consciousness focused on the astral. Work in the upper astral realms or magical planes is particularly useful for artists, as it opens a creative channel that has its manifestation on the physical plane. Dion Fortune refers to this particular phenomenon as "The Green Ray," and associates it specifically with Druidic initiation and their arts of poetry and music, as well as the arts of the Golden Age of Greece and their initiatory mysteries.

Before you conclude an astral working, always remember to reabsorb any symbols you have been using back into yourself before ending the session (such as weapons, tatwas or other tools). It is easy enough to formulate them again once they have been firmly established in your psyche. It is both dangerous and sloppy to leave personal symbols on the astral plane.

You must be extremely careful to bring your Astral Body back to your physical body. This is known in popular parlance as "grounding." I have found Crowley's instructions to be the simplest and most effective. Bring the astral body back to correspond with the location of the physical body, and vibrate the name of Harpocrates while assuming his god form (an erect posture with the right forefinger pressed to the lips in the Sign of Silence, see page 133). Take care to completely ground yourself after each session even if your session has not seemed particularly successful or "real." Symptoms of unsuccessful "grounding" include headache, dizziness, overwhelming fatigue, nausea, sudden irrational irritability, general "spaciness" and nightmares. Crowley and Fortune also list paralysis and madness as negative side-effects of unsuccessful or incomplete astral journeys. Drugs and alcohol abuse often coincide with sloppy astral practices.

When you are thoroughly satisfied that you have grounded yourself and your consciousness has returned to the physical plane, perform a banishing ritual, and record your experience in your magical diary.

Basics of Pathworking and a Simple Example

The basic steps to a successful Pathworking are as follows:
- Setting up the workspace
- Banishing
- Preliminary Invocation
- Astral Projection
- "Walking the Path"
- Resolution
- Grounding
- Banishing
- Recording the Experience
- Integration

When a person thinks of Pathworking, one automatically thinks of the actual paths joining the Sephiroth on the Tree of Life. Actually, you start your operation at the Sephiroth directly "below" the path you will be working. *Aleister Crowley's Treasure House of Images* is a great tool to use to successfully invoke the energy of the Path with which you are working.

For the purposes of an example, I'd like to use the Path connecting Yesod and Tiphareth. This is the path of Samekh, attributed to the Tarot card "Art" (also called Temperance) and the zodiacal sign Sagittarius. So, for this exercise we will be travelling the path of Samekh, but we will begin in Yesod and (hopefully) end in Tiphareth. Prior to starting–during the days and maybe weeks prior, the first thing I usually do is to write down and recall all the correspondences to this path I can think of. I then consult Crowley's *777* to gather even more information. I also read and (optimally) memorize the chapter in *The Treasure House of Images* associated with the path. I also gather any props or materials I will need for the operation.

For the Pathworking

1. Arrange the temple with the necessary symbols and tools to aid you on your journey. Stage your space creatively, so that it is significant for

you an what you hope to accomplish. For example, you may wish to place an image of one of the deities of the Path listed in 777–Nepthy, Diana, Artemis or Apollo–and an image of the Art card, Atu XIV. I would put an arrow on my altar also, because it is the magical weapon associated with the path. Color association is important for me–and the colors associated with this path are Blue (King Scale), Yellow (Queen Scale), Green (Prince Scale), and Dark Vivid Blue (Princess Scale).

2. Do a thorough banishing–again I would recommend at least a Lesser Banishing Ritual of the Pentagram. I tend to perform the Star Ruby as well (for full instructions on this, as well as many other rituals, please refer to *Magick* by Aleister Crowley).

3. Light incense appropriate to your working. Since we are focusing on the Path of Samekh, I would recommend a Lignum Aloes blend. Invoke the energy of the Path by reciting aloud the "Sagittarius" chapter associated with it, called "The Chapter known as The Twelvefold Rejoicing of God and the Unity thereof." Pay close attention and let the words sink into your psyche as much as possible. It is infinitely better if you have the relevant chapter memorized, so the vivid imagery of the hymns are embedded in your subconscious. You will need to recall these images later in your working.

4. Settle yourself into a comfortable position, and start to focus on your breathing. As you become more aware of the patterns of your breath, your body will start to relax and open. At the same time, your mind will become more focused and sensitive to the subtle energies circulating within your breath. When you are ready, become aware of your subtle body and start to transfer your consciousness into that part of yourself. Finally, switch yourself over into your astral form. Your physical body will remain safe and relaxed.

5. Your astral body will continue to rise until you reach a temple space. This space will be the sphere from which you are starting your journey. In this case it is Yesod, the Sphere of Luna. Not what the space looks like. What is its shape? What colors are here? What types of beings populate this space? Do you see Heirophantic or Kerubic images? After you

peruse the space, you should open the Temple for your working. You can do this in a number of ways (with a word, sign or sigil appropriate to the Sephiroth for example). For Yesod, something appropriate would be to use the magical formula ALIM along with a Hexagram invoking the Planetary Energy. At this point, you should do something appropriate to please the ruler of the sphere. This can be as simple as vibrating the god name of the sphere (in Yesod, it would be *Shaddai El Chai*). After you establish your right to be in the Sphere, inscribe the appropriate invoking Hexagram. For the purposes of this example, you should use the hexagram of Jupiter, because Jupiter rules Sagittarius. (See page 128.) At this point, a portal into the Path should appear. You may or may not be approached by a being who can guide you in the experience of the Path. If you find yourself in the company of a being, make sure to question them carefully. If you find he cannot answer the questions in an appropriate manner or disregards/ ignores your question, banish him immediately. You can invoke again to see if you can find the correct guide or you can explore the Path on your own. Spend time soaking in the experience of the Path you are on. Take note of the beings, symbol sets, and themes you find there. Keep an open mind and treat all beings you meet there firmly, but courteously. Question these beings as much as you can and banish those not belonging there.

All paths have unique points of significance. On the path in our example, Samekh, during your exploration you will notice a shimmering object on the path in front of you. As you come closer, you will realize it is a barrier of highly reflective material. You may actually see yourself reflected back at you. This is the Veil of Paroketh, the veil of illusion between the ego and the higher self. We are drawn towards this veil–it is the pull of the Soul towards the Ego. It is a pull we all experience. As it is written in *The Book of the Law*, "For I am divided for love's sake, for the chance of union." Some magical groups say that the Veil of Paroketh embodies the Four Powers of the Sphinx–*Scire, Velle, Audere, Tacere*–and that to pierce the veil, one must possess a fifth power, Ire, which means "To Go." Do you have that quality within you? Are you ready to travel beyond the veil? If you don't think so, what tools do you need to acquire? You could stop here and carefully question your guide or any type of guardian spirit (that you may find sitting motionless to the right of the veil). If you decide to end your travels here, allow yourself to descend to the physical plane. See numbers 7-10 below for the correct sequence. If you travel on through the veil, note any changes in perception after you've crossed through the barrier. Note who or what you find on this part of the Path. What can you learn from them? What can you learn from yourself?

6. At the end of the Path, you will arrive in another, "higher" Sepiroth. Take good note of what types of magical images you find there. What Guardians and/or Keribim are present? Make sure to do something to assure the Guardians of the Sephiroth. Again, you can vibrate an appropriate magical formula of the Sphere (in our example, we end at Tiphareth, so you could use the god name *Jehovah Eloah va-Daath*. Pay close attention to the images and symbols in this sphere. Listen carefully to anything the beings inhabiting this sphere may have to say to you. Carefully explore everything you can perceive in the Sphere. When you are finished, you should close the temple space. You would perform the appropriate banishing ritual of the Hexagram of Jupiter (see *Liber O*) after absorbing any tools you may be carrying with you.

7. Allow your astral body to descend slowly back to earth and gently shift your consciousness back into your physical body. Place your right forefinger over your lips and assume the God-Form of Harpocrates. Slowly open your eyes.

8. Perform a thorough Banishing Ritual.

9. Carefully record your experiences.

10. In the days and weeks following this exercise, you may notice certain corresponding synchronous events occurring in your life. For example, the magical power of the path of Samekh is "transmutation." You may find yourself in a different job or, having passed through the Veil of Paroketh, you may find you have a new outlook on an old partnership. Or you may notice that you keep seeing the same symbols you found during the Pathworking in magazine ads or in works of art. Make a note of these synchronicities in your magical diary.

Pay attention to your dreams and try to become more active, rather than passive.

Pathworking is a dynamic and ever changing art. It offers endless possibilities for exploring the interior spaces of the psyche and soul. It is a relatively simple approach to the complex astral universe. With a little practice, it is a tool anyone can take advantage of and use for self improvement.

Additional Tips

1. It's important to pay attention to your physical health when building your Body of Light. It is very hard to build the astral body into the properly formed weapon a magician requires if the physical and/or mental bodies are in shambles. Keep the mind disciplined and the physical body strong and supple. Hatha Yoga is an excellent way to both tone the body and calm the mind. If your physical body is weak, so will your astral body be. If you are sensitive enough to read auras, you know you can often sense when a person is ill or tired. Never attempt Pathworking or any other type of astral work if you are sick or run down. Not only could your physical body suffer, but you will also be more vulnerable to psychic attack and you will not be able to function as efficiently. In the long run, it is probably better to wait to do Pathworking when you are feeling physically strong and rested.

2. Keep a tight rein on the imagination and explore the astral plane logically, with discrimination, objectivity and care. It is easy to succumb to the desires and dreams of your imagination; this is the beginner's greatest danger. If you surround yourself on the astral with products of your own imagination, it becomes impossible to achieve real results. While imaginary experiences may seem very real, they lead, at best, to inconvenience when you realize you've been duping yourself and must therefore retrain. At worst, your psyche could be in real peril and in danger of destruction. Meeting a real, outside-yourself entity on the astral plane is unmistakable. It leaves a lasting impression and effects some change in your consciousness. Again, this is where knowledge of the Kabbalah is very useful.

3. Another danger of Pathworking is obsession. It is important to pay very close attention to your day-to-day life while doing this sort of work. If you find yourself at work or school consumed by the desire to run home and escape to the astral plane or perform another Pathworking, things could be seriously amiss. On the other hand, if you are performing a series of formal Pathworkings, or training under the auspices of an initiatory/training school, or working with a teacher, it is important to reflect on experiences gained during previous working, and to plot out subsequent workings. However, it is extremely easy to slip into a fantasy world. Astral workings are not to be used as an escape from reality. Positive results of astral working should result in a richer experience, enjoyment and comprehension of the physical plane.

4. Pay particular attention to your dreams during any meditation series, Pathworking, or astral workings. Keep a dream diary. Take advantage of your dreams and try deliberate projection while dreaming. Learn to shape your dreams.

The Sign of Enterer (Blind Force)

Liber O

vel Manus Et Sagittae
sub figura VI

Aleister Crowley
from *The Equinox*, Vol. I, No. 2

I

1. This book is very easy to misunderstand; readers are asked to use the most minute critical care in the study of it, even as we have done in its preparation.

2. In this book it is spoken of the Sephiroth and the Paths; of Spirit and Conjurations; of Gods, Spheres, Planes, and many other things which may or may not exist.

It is immaterial whether these exist or not. By doing certain things certain results will follow; students are most earnestly warned against attributing objective reality or philosophic validity to any of them.

3. The advantages to be gained from them are chiefly these:
   (a) A widening of the horizon of the mind.
   (b) An improvement of the control of the mind.

4. The student, if he attains any success in the following practices, will find himself confronted by things (ideas or beings) too glorious or too dreadful to be described. It is essential that he remain the master of all that he beholds, hears or conceives; otherwise he will be the slave of illusion, and the prey of madness.

Before entering upon any of these practices, the student should be in good health, and have attained a fair mastery of Asana, Pranayama and Dharana.

5. There is little danger that any student, however idle or stupid, will fail to get some results; but there is great danger that he will be led astray, obsessed and overwhelmed by his results, even though it be by those which it is necessary that he should attain. Too often, moreover, he mistaketh the first resting-place for the goal, and taketh off his armour as if he were a victor ere the fight is well begun.

It is desirable that the student should never attach to any result the importance which it at first seems to possess.

6. First, then, let us consider the Book 777 and it use; the preparation of the Place; the use of the Magic Ceremonies; and finally the methods which follow in Chapter V "Viator in Regnis Arboris," and in Chapter VI "Sagitta trans Lunam."

(In another book will it be treated of the Expansion and Contraction of Consciousness; progress by slaying the Chakrams; progress by slaying the Pairs of Opposites; the methods of Sabhapaty Swami, etc., etc.)

II

1. The student must first obtain a thorough knowledge of Book 777, especially of columns i, ii, iii, v, vi, vii, ix, xi, xii, xiv, sv, svi, svii, sviii, xix, xxxiv, xxxv, xxxviii, xxxix, xl, sli, slii, slv, liv, lv, lix, lx, lxi, lxiii, lxx, lxxv, lxxvii, lxxviii, lxxix, lxxx, lxxxi, lxxxiii, xcvii, xcviii, xcix, c, ci, cxvii, cxviii, xcccvii, cxxxviii, cxxxix, clxxv, clxxvi, clxxvii, clxxxii.

When these are committed to memory, he will begin to understand the nature of these correspondences. (See illustrations "The Temple of Solomon the King" [Equinox 1, 2].

2. If we take an example, the use of the table will become clear.

Let us suppose that you wish to obtain knowledge of some obscure science.

In column xlv, line 12, you will find "Knowledge of Sciences."

By now looking up line 12 in the other columns, you will find that the Planet corresponding is Mercury, its number eight, its lineal figures the octagon and octagram. The God who rules that planet Thoth, or in Hebrew symbolism Tetragrammaton Adonai and Elohim Tzabaoth, its Archangel Raphael, its Choir of Angels Beni Elohim, its Intelligence Tiriel, its Spirit Taphtatharath, its colours Orange (for Mercury is the Sphere of the Sephira Hod, 8), Yellow, Purple, Grey, and Indigo rayed with Violet; its Magical Weapon the Wand of Caduceus, its Perfumes Mastic and others, its sacred plants Vervain and others, its jewel the Opal or Agate; its sacred animal the Snake, etc., etc.,

3. You would then prepare your Place of Working accordingly. In an orange circle you would draw an eight-pointed star of yellow, at whose points you would place eight lamps. The Sigil of the Spirit (which is to be found in Cornelius Agrippa and other books) you would draw in the four colours with such other devices as your experience may suggest.

4. And so on. We cannot here enter at length into all the necessary preparations; and the student will find them fully set forth in the proper books, of which the *Goetia* is perhaps the best example.

These rituals need not be slavishly imitated; on the contrary the student should do nothing the object of which he does not understand; also, if he have any capacity whatever, he will find his own crude rituals more effective than the highly polished ones of other people.

The general purpose of all this preparation is as follows:

5. Since the student is a man surrounded by material objects, if it be his wish to master one particular idea, he must make every material object about him directly suggest that idea. Thus in the ritual quoted, if his glance fall upon the limits, their number suggests Mercury; he smells the perfumes, and again Mercury is brought to his mind. In other words, the whole magical apparatus and ritual is a complex system of mnemonics.

116 Aleister Crowley's Treasure House of Images

(The importance of these lies principally in the fact that particular sets of images that the student may meet in his wanderings correspond to particular lineal figures, divine names, etc. and are controlled by them. As to the possibility of producing results external to the mind of the seer [objective, in the ordinary common sense acceptation of the term] we are here silent.)

6. There are three important practices connected with all forms of ceremonial (and the two Methods which later we shall describe). These are:

(1) Assumption of God-forms.

(2) Vibration of Divine Names.

(3) Rituals of "Banishing" and "Invoking."

These, at least, should be completely mastered before the dangerous Methods of Chapters V and VI are attempted.

III

1. The Magical Images of the Gods of Egypt should be made thoroughly familiar. This can be done by studying them in any public museum, or in such books as may be accessible to the student. They should then be carefully painted by him, both from the model and from memory.

2. The student, seated in the "God" position, or in the characteristic attitude of the God desired, should then imagine His image as coinciding with his own body, or as enveloping it. This must be practised until mastery of the image is attained, and an identity with it and with the God experienced.

It is a matter for very regret that no simple and certain test of success in this practice exists.

3. The Vibration of God-names. As a further means of identifying the human consciousness with that pure portion of it which man calls by the name of some God, let him act thus:

4. (a) Stand with arms outstretched.[1] (*See* illustration [p. 123].)

---

[1] This injunction does not apply to gods like Phthah or Harpocrates whose natures do not accord with this gesture.

(b) Breathe in deeply through the nostrils, imagining the name of the God desired entering with the breath.

(c) Let that name descend slowly from the lungs to the heart, the solar plexus, the navel, the generative organs, and so to the feet.

(d) The moment that it appears to touch the feet, quickly advance the left foot about 12 inches, throw forward the body, and let the hands (drawn back to the side of the eyes) shoot out, so that you are standing in the typical position of the God Horus,[2] and at the same time imagine the Name as rushing up and through the body, while you breathe it out through the nostrils with the air which has been till then retained in the lungs. All this must be done with all the force of which you are capable.

(e) Then withdraw the left foot, and place the right forefinger[3] upon the lips, so that you are in the characteristic position of the God Harpocrates.[4]

5. It is a sign that the student is performing this correctly when a single "Vibration" entirely exhausts his physical strength. It should cause him to grow hot all over, or to perspire violently, and it should so weaken him that he will find it difficult to remain standing.

6. It is a sign of success, though only by the student himself is it perceived, when he hears the name of the God vehemently roared forth, as if by the concourse of ten thousand thunders; and it should appear to him as if that Great Voice proceeded from the Universe, and not from himself.

In both the above practices all consciousness of anything but the God-form and name should be absolutely blotted out; and the longer it takes for normal perception to return; the better.

---

[2] *See* illustration "Blind Force," [p. 124].
[3] Or the thumb, the fingers being closed. The thumb symbolises spirit, the forefinger the element of water.
[4] *See* illustration "Silent Watcher," [p. 143].

IV

1. The Rituals of the Pentagram and Hexagram must be committed to memory. They are as follows:

The Lesser Ritual of the Pentagram

- (i) Touching the forehead say Ateh (Unto Thee).
- (ii) Touching the breast say Malkuth (The Kingdom).
- (iii) Touching the right shoulder, say ve-Geburah (and the Power).
- (iv) Touching the left shoulder, say ve-Gedulah (and the Glory).
- (v) Clasping the hands upon the breast, say le-Olahm, Amen (to the Ages, Amen).
- (vi) Turning the East make a pentagram (that of Earth) with the proper weapon (usually the Wand). Say (i.e., vibrate) I H V H.
- (vii) Turning to the South, the same, but say A D N I.
- (viii) Turning to the West, the same, but say A H I H.
- (ix) Turning to the North, the same, but say A G L A. Pronounce: Ye-ho-wau, Adonai, Eheieh, Agla.
- (x) Extending the arms in the form of a Cross say:
- (xi) Before me Raphael;
- (xii) Behind me Gabriel;
- (xiii) On my right hand Michael;
- (xiv) On my left hand Auriel;
- (xv) For about me flames the Pentagram,
- (xvi) And in the Column stands the six-rayed Star.
- (xvii-xxi) Repeat (i) to (v), the Qabalistic Cross.

The Greater Ritual of the Pentagram

The Pentagrams are traced in the air with the sword or other weapon, the name spoken aloud, and the signs used, as illustrated.

THE PENTAGRAMS OF SPIRIT

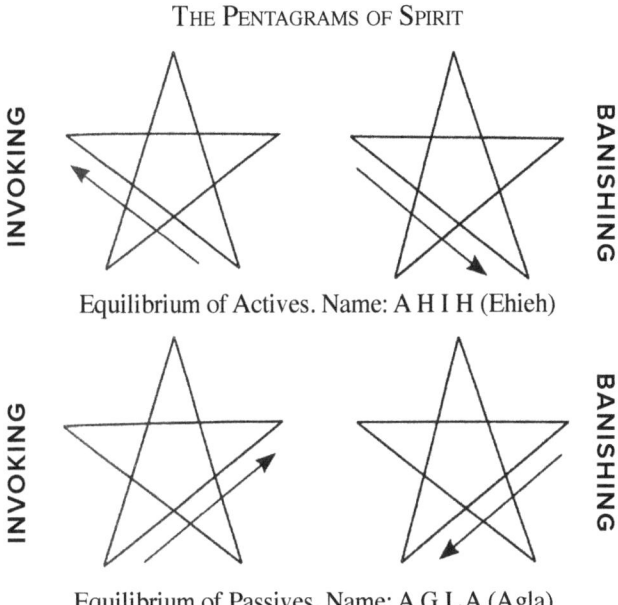

Equilibrium of Actives. Name: A H I H (Ehieh)

Equilibrium of Passives. Name: A G L A (Agla)

The Signs of the Portal (*see* illustrations [page 122]): Extend the hands in front of you, palms outwards, separate them as if in the act of rending asunder a veil or curtain (actives), and then bring them together as if closing it up again and let them fall to the side (passives).

(The Grade of the "Portal" is particularly attributed to the element of Spirit; it refers to the Sun; the Paths of ס, ר, and צ, are attributed to this degree. See *777* lines 6 and 31 bis).

THE PENTAGRAMS OF FIRE

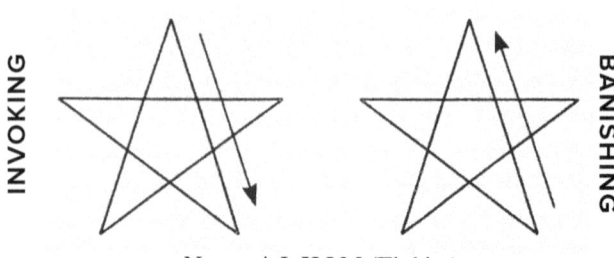

Name: A L H I M (Elohim)

The signs of 4°=7▫: Raise the arms above the head and join the hands, so that the tips of the fingers and of the thumbs meet, formulating a triangle. (*See* illustration.)

The signs of 4°=7▫ is particularly attributed to the element Fire; it refers to the planet Venus; the paths of ק, צ, and פ are attributed to this degree. For other attributions *see 777* lines 7 and 31).

THE PENTAGRAMS OF FIRE

Name: A L (El)

The signs of 3°=8▫: Raise the arms above till the elbows are on the level with the shoulders, bring the hands across the chest, touching the thumbs and tips of fingers so as to form a triangle apex downwards. (*See* illustration.)

The signs of 3°=8▫ is particularly attributed to the element of Water; it refers to the planet Mercury; the paths of ר and ש are attributed to this degree. For other attributions *see 777,* lines 8 and 23).

The Signs of the Grades

1. Earth: the god Set fighting.

2. Air: the god Shu supporting the sky.

3. Water: the goddess Auramoth

4. Fire: the goddess Thoum-aesh-neith

5-6. Spirit: the rending and closing of the veil.

7-10 THE LVX SIGNS

7. + Osiris slain–the Cross

8. L Isis mourning–the Svastika

9. V Typhon–the Trident

10. X Osiris risen–the Pentagram

The Pentagrams of Air

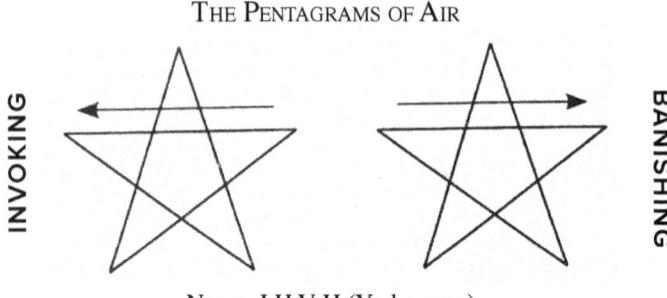

Name: I H V H (Ye-ho-wau)

The signs of 2°=9☐: Stretch both arms upwards and outwards, the elbows bent at right angles, the hands bent back, the palms upwards as if supporting a weight. (*See* illustration.)

The Grade of 2°=9☐ is particularly attributed to the element Air; it refers to the Moon; the path of ה is attributed to this degree. For other attributions *see* 777 lines 9 and 11).

The Pentagrams of Earth

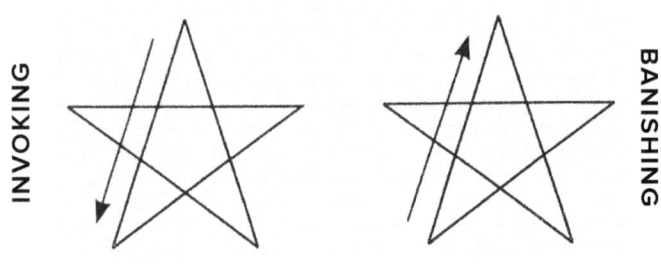

Name: A D N I (Adonai)

The signs of 1°=10☐: Advance the right foot, stretch out the right hand upwards and forwards, the left hand downwards and backwards, the palms open. (*See* illustration.)

(The Grade of 1°=10☐ is particularly attributed to the element of Earth, *see* 777, lines 10 and 32 bis).

The Lesser Ritual of the Hexagram

This ritual is to be performed after the "Lesser Ritual of the Pentagram."

- (i) Stand upright, feet together, left arm at side, right across body, holding the wand or other weapon upright in the median line. Then face East and say:
- (ii) I.N.R.I.
  Yod. Nun. Resh. Yod.
  Virgo, Isis, Mighty Mother.
  Scorpio, Apophis, Destroyer.
  Sol, Osiris, Slain and Risen.
  Isis, Apophis, Osiris, IAO.
- (iii) Extend the arms in the form of a cross, and say: "The Sign of Osiris Slain." (*See* illustration).
- (iv) Raise the right arm to point upwards, keeping the elbow square, and lower the left arm to point downwards, keeping the elbow square, while turning the head over the left shoulder looking down so that the eyes follow the left forearm, and say, "The Sign of the Mourning of Isis." (*See* illustration).
- (v) Raise the arms at an angle of sixty degrees to each other above the head, which is thrown back, and say, "The Sign of Apophis and Typhon." (*See* illustration).
- (vi) Cross the arms on the breast, and bow the head and say, "The Sign of Osiris Risen. (*See* illustration).
- (vii) Extend the arms again as in (iii) and cross them again as in (vi) saying: "L.V.X., Lux, the Light of the Cross."

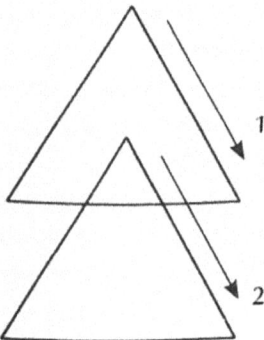

(viii) With the magical weapon trace the Hexagram of Fire in the East, saying "Ararita"
This word consists of the initials of a sentence which means "One is His Beginning: One is His Individuality: His Permutation is One."

The hexagram consists of two equilateral triangles, both apices pointed upwards. Begin at the top of the upper triangle and trace it in a destrorotary direction. The top of the lower triangle should coincide with the central point of the upper triangle.

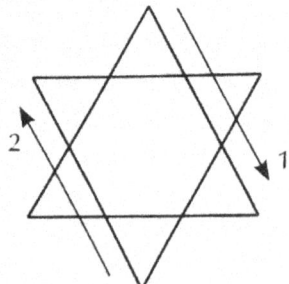

(ix) Trace the Hexagram of Earth in the South, saying "ARARITA." This Hexagram has the apex of the lower triangle pointing downwards, and it should be capable of inscription in a circle.

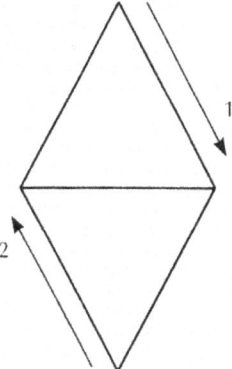

(x) Trace the Hexagram of Air in the West, saying ARARITA." This Hexagram is like that of Earth; but the bases of the triangles coincide, forming a diamond.

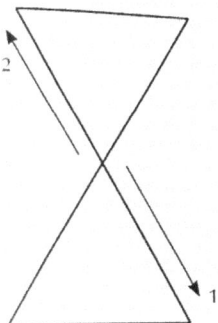

(xi) Trace the Hexagram of Water in the North, saying ARARITA." This hexagram is the lower triangle placed above the upper, so that their apices coincide.

(xii) Repeat (i-vii)

The Banishing Ritual is identical, save that the direction of the Hexagrams must be reversed.

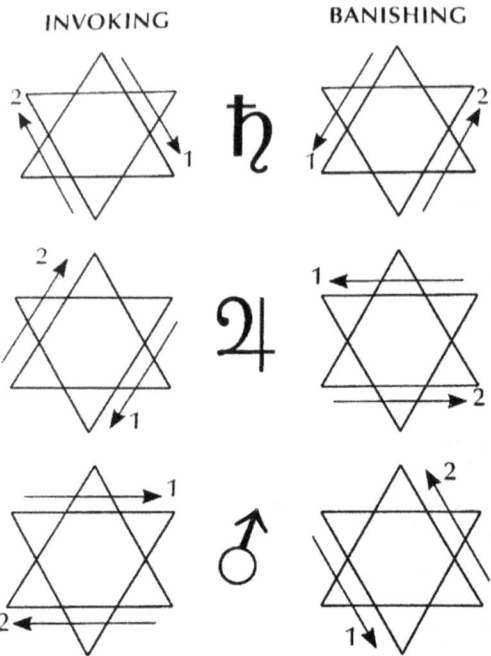

To invoke or banish planets or zodiacal signs.

The Hexagrams of Earth alone is used. Draw the hexagram, beginning from the point which is attributed to the planet you are dealing with. (*See 777* col. lxxxiii).

Thus to invoke Jupiter begin from the right-hand point of the lower triangle, dextro-rotary and complete; then trace the upper triangle from its left hand point and complete.

Trace the astrological sigil of the planet in the centre of your hexagram.

For the Zodiac use the hexagram of the planet which rules the sign you require (*see 777*, col. cxxxviii); but draw the astrological sigil of the sign, instead of that of the planet.

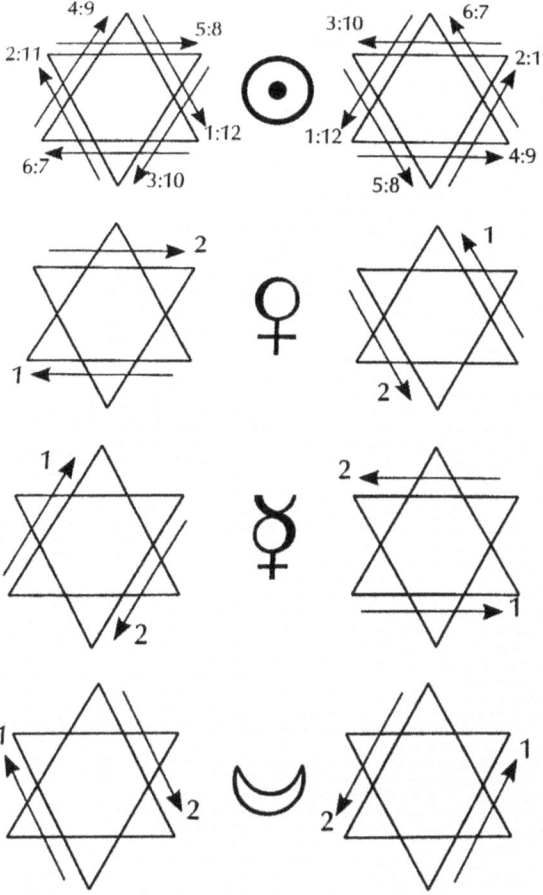

For Caput and Cauda Draconis use the lunar hexagram, with the sigil of ☊ or ☋.

To banish, reverse the hexagram.

In all cases use a conjuration first with Ararita, and next with the name of the God corresponding to the planter or sign you are dealing with.

The Hexagrams pertaining to the planets are as in plates above and on the preceding page.

2. These rituals should be practised until the figures drawn appear in flame, in flame so near to physical flame that it would perhaps be visible to the eyes of a bystander, were one present. It is alleged that some persons have attained the power of actually kindling fire by these means. Whether this be so or not, the power is not one to be aimed at.

3. Success in "banishing" is known by a "feeling of cleanliness" in the atmosphere; success in "invoking" by a "feeling of holiness." It is unfortunate that these terms are so vague.

But at least make sure of this: that any imaginary figure or being shall instantly obey the will of the student, when he uses the appropriate figure. In obstinate cases, the form of the appropriate God may be assumed.

4. The banishing rituals should be used at the commencement of any ceremony whatever. Next, the student should use a general invocation, such as the "Preliminary Invocation" in the *Goetia* as well as a special invocation to suit the nature of his working.

5. Success in these verbal invocations is so subtle a matter, and its grades so delicately shaded, that it must be left to the good sense of a student to decide whether or not he should be satisfied with his result.

V

1. Let the student be at rest in one of his prescribed positions, having bathed and robed with the proper decorum. Let the place of working be free from all disturbance, and let the preliminary purifications, banishings and invocations be duly accomplished, and, lastly, let the incense be kindled.

2. Let him imagine his own figure (preferably robed in the proper magical garments and armed with the proper magical weapons) as enveloping his physical body, or standing near to and in front of him.

3. Let him then transfer the seat of his consciousness to that imagined figure; so that it may seem to him that he is seeing with its eyes, and hearing with its ears.

4. Let him then cause that imagined figure to rise in the air to a great height above the earth.

5. Let him then stop and look about him. (It is sometimes difficult to open the eyes.)

6. Probably he will see figures approaching him, or become conscious of a landscape.

Let him speak to such figures, and insist upon being answered, using the proper pentagrams and signs, as previously taught.

7. Let him travel about at will, either with or without guidance from such figure or figures.

8. Let him further employ such special invocations as will cause to appear the particular places he may wish to visit.

9. Let him beware of the thousand subtle attacks and deceptions tha the will experience, carefully testing the truth of all with whom he speaks.

Thus a hostile being may appear clothed with glory; the appropriate pentagram will in such a case cause him to shrival or decay.

10. Practice will make the student infinitely wary in these matters.

11. It is usually quite easy to return to the body, but should any difficulty arise, practice (again) will make the imagination fertile. For example, one may create in thought a chariot of fire with white horses, and command the charioteer to drive earthwards.

It might be dangerous to go too far, or to stay too long; for fatigue must be avoided.

The danger spoken of is that of fainting, or of obsession, or of loss of memory or other mental faculty.

12. Finally, let the student cause his imagined body in which he supposes himself to have been travelling to coincide with the physical, tightening his muscles, drawing in his breath, and putting his forefinger to his lips. Then let him "awake" by a well-defined act of will, and soberly and accurately record his experiences.

It may be added that this apparently complicated experiment is perfectly easy to perform. It is best to learn by "travelling" with a person already experienced in the matter. Two or three experiments will suffice to render the student confident and even expert. See also "The Seer," [*The Equinox* I, 2] pp. 295-333.

VI

1. The previous experiment has little value, and leads to few results of importance. But it is susceptible of a development which merges into a form of Dharana–concentration–and as such may lead to the very highest ends. The principal use of the practice in the last chapter is to familiarise the student with every kind of obstacle and every kind of delusion, so that he may be perfect master of every idea that may arise in his brain, to dismiss it, to transmute it, to cause it instantly to obey his will.

2. Let him then begin exactly as before, but with the most intense solemnity and determination.

3. Let him be very careful to cause his imaginary body to rise in a line exactly perpendicular to the earth's tangent at the point where his physical body is situated (or to put it more simply, straight upwards).

4. Instead of stopping, let him continue to rise until fatigue almost overcomes him. If he should find that he has stopped without willing to do so, and that figures appear, let him at all costss rise above them.

Yea, though his very life tremble on his lips, let him force his way upward and onward!

5. Let him continue in this so long as the breath of life is in him. Whatever threatens, whatever allures, though it were Typhon and all his hosts loosed from the pit and leagued against him, though it were from the very Throne of God Himself that a Voice issues bidding him stay and be content, let him struggle on, ever on.

6. At last there must come a moment when his whole being is swallowed up in fatigue, overwhelmed by its own inertia.[5]

Let him sink (when no longer can he strive, though his tongue by bitten through with the effort and the blood gush from his nostrils) into the blackness of unconciousness; and then, on coming to himself, let him write down soberly and accurately a record of all that hath occurred, yea a record of all that hath occurred.

EXPLICIT

---

[5] This in case of failure. The results of success are so many and wonderful that no effort is here made to describe them. They are classified, tentatively, in the "*Herb Dangerous*," Part II, [*The Equinox* 1, 2].

The Sign of Silence

New Falcon Publications
Publisher of Controversial Books and CDs
Invites You to Visit Our Website:
http://www.newfalcon.com

At the Falcon website you can:

- Browse the online catalog of all our great titles, including books by Robert Anton Wilson, Christopher S. Hyatt, Israel Regardie, Aleister Crowley, Timothy Leary, Osho, Lon Milo DuQuette and many more
- Find out what's available and what's out of stock
- Get special discounts
- Order our titles through our secure online server
- Find products not available anywhere else including:
    - One of a kind and limited availability products
    - Special packages
    - Special pricing
- And much, much more

Get online today at http://www.newfalcon.com